LORDS, LADIES, PEASANTS, AND KNIGHTS:
CLASS IN THE MIDDLE AGES

Lords, Ladies, Peasants, and Knights:
Class in the Middle Ages

DON NARDO

LUCENT BOOKS

An imprint of Thomson Gale, a part of The Thomson Corporation

Detroit • New York • San Francisco • San Diego • New Haven, Conn. • Waterville, Maine • London • Munich

LIBRARY OF CONGRESS CATALOGING-IN-PUBLICATION DATA

Nardo, Don, 1947–
    Lords, ladies, peasants, and knights: class in the Middle Ages / by Don Nardo.
        p. cm. — (The Lucent library of historical eras. Middle Ages)
    Includes bibliographical references and index.
    ISBN 1-59018-928-0 (hard cover : alk. paper) 1. Social classes—Europe—History—
To 1500—Juvenile literature. 2. Social structure—Europe—History—To 1500—
Juvenile literature. 3. Civilization, Medieval—Juvenile literature. I. Title. II. Series.
    HN380.Z9S6456 2006
    305.5094'0902—dc22
                                                                    2006007162

Printed in the United States of America

Contents

Foreword

Looking back from the vantage point of the present, history can be viewed as a myriad of intertwining roads paved by human events. Some paths stand out—broad highways whose mileposts, even from a distance of centuries, are clear. The events that propelled the rise to power of Germany's Third Reich, its role in World War II, and its eventual demise, for example, are well defined and documented.

Other roads are less distinct, their route sometimes hidden from view. Modern legislatures may have developed from old tribal councils, for example, but the links between them are indistinct in places, open to discussion and interpretation.

The architecture of civilization—law, religion, art, science, and government—as well as the more everyday aspects of our culture—what we eat, what we wear—all developed along the historical roads and byways. In that progression can be traced every facet of modern life.

A broad look back along these roads reveals that many paths—though of vastly different character—seem to converge at a few critical junctions. These intersections are those great historical eras that echo over the long, steady course of human history, extending beyond the past and into the present.

These epic periods of time are the focus of Lucent's Library of Historical Eras. They shine through the mists of history like beacons, illuminated by a burst of creativity that propels events forward—so bright that we, from thousands of years away, can clearly see the chain of events leading to the present.

Each Lucent Library of Historical Eras consists of a set of books that highlight various aspects of these major eras. For example, the Elizabethan England library features volumes on Queen Elizabeth I and her court, Elizabethan theater, the great playwrights, and everyday life in Elizabethan London.

The mini-library approach allows for the division of each era into its most significant and most interesting parts and the exploration of those parts in depth.

Also, social and cultural trends as well as illustrative documents and eyewitness accounts can be prominently featured in individual volumes.

Lucent's Library of Historical Eras presents a wealth of information to young readers. The lively narrative, fully documented primary and secondary source quotations, maps, photographs, sidebars, and annotated bibliographies serve as launching points for class discussion and further research.

In studying the great historical eras, students also develop a better understanding of our own times. What we learn from the past and how we apply it in the present may shape the future and may determine whether our era will be a guiding light to those traveling future roads.

Introduction

MEDIEVAL PEOPLE: THE HARSH REALITIES OF THEIR WORLD

Modern Western society has long been fascinated by European medieval society and the medieval era, also known as the Middle Ages. No one living during this thousand-year period actually called it by this name: The term *medieval* derives from the Latin phrase *medium aevum*, meaning "the age in the middle." Modern historians came to view the medieval era as the period that separated ancient times from modern times and date it from about A.D. 500 to 1600, roughly from the fall of Rome to the end of the Renaissance.

The strong modern interest in the Middle Ages is reflected in the huge number of popular books, movies, television shows, and even video games with medieval themes. Among the images that have become iconic and instantly recognizable as medieval are stone castles with moats and drawbridges, heavily armored knights charging on horseback, Gothic cathedrals with spires reaching toward the heavens, heroic quests, and spiritual pilgrimages.

Links Between Past and Present

These images of the past may be quaint and romanticized. What brings them fully to life for the reader or viewer is something people everywhere can relate to, namely, the experiences of fellow human beings no matter how different their circumstances. Behind the familiar images that symbolize the medieval era are the real people who played vital roles in medieval society. A castle, for example, was not simply an imposing building. More importantly, it was the home of a king or other noble as well as his family, servants, and the soldiers who guarded the premises. Within each cathedral, country chapel, or monastery dwelled priests, monks, or nuns. And in nearby towns merchants, shopkeepers, public officials, scholars, artisans, and laborers lived and worked. Meanwhile, the long and winding dirt roads that connected the castles, churches, and towns were traversed by traders, soldiers, religious pilgrims, and wandering entertainers, as well as robbers and other disreputable characters.

Modern observers can relate to these characters through the universality of the human experience, which transcends time and place. In the act of peering into a past world, people recognize basic situations, emotions, and dilemmas similar to their

An illustration in a fourteenth-century French manuscript shows European knights capturing the fortress-town of Acre in Palestine during the Second Crusade.

own. For instance, the medieval father who forbade his daughter to marry beneath her social class or outside of her religion has counterparts in many modern societies. And today some men and women still choose to serve their god by taking vows of chastity and poverty and living in quiet monasteries.

Profound Differences Between Past and Present

Despite these and other similarities, however, the people of the present and the people of the medieval past remain separated by a vast cultural and logistical gulf. On one level, these cultural differences now appear fascinating, colorful, even inspiring. Many modern enthusiasts see the medieval era as a time of antique storybook costumes; chivalry and honor among warriors; charming, romantic rituals of love and courtship; and the splendor of ornate palaces and royal courts populated by bearded lords and elegant ladies-in-waiting.

There are elements of truth in all of these pleasant images. But it would be profoundly misleading to imagine that the lives of medieval people were more pleasant than the lives of people today. Overall, in fact, the realities of life in the Middle Ages were a good deal more unpleasant, uncomfortable, unpredictable, and downright dangerous.

Indeed, by measures of creature comforts alone, life today is far more amenable. Medieval castles and houses had no central heating; the only way to stay warm indoors in the winter was to huddle around a fireplace and/or wear many layers of clothes. There was no electric light or power, and thus no such thing as radio, TV, computers and other electronic media, no refrigeration, no air-conditioning, and no electric appliances of any kind. To see and function at night, people had to rely on candles, torches, and oil lamps. Also, there were no flush toilets, running water, or other advanced plumbing features that are taken for granted today. Instead, people used buckets to carry water indoors and laboriously filled washbasins and bathtubs by hand.

Moreover, the water transported with such difficulty came directly from lakes and streams. It was not filtered and cleaned, as the water in most modern Western towns is, and there was no way to tell what human, animal, or other contaminants lurked in the water. People were surrounded by and regularly handled or inhaled other noxious substances as well. It was common, for instance, to keep human and animal waste in buckets or barrels inside the house. When these containers were full, people dumped them into street gutters, backyard manure piles, ponds, and streams. Those with separate outhouses also dumped their accumulated waste outside in piles. Often, the sun dried the manure into a powder, which the wind blew over villages and houses and into open windows.

Ravaged by Disease

Often related to this general and appalling lack of sanitation was the abysmal state

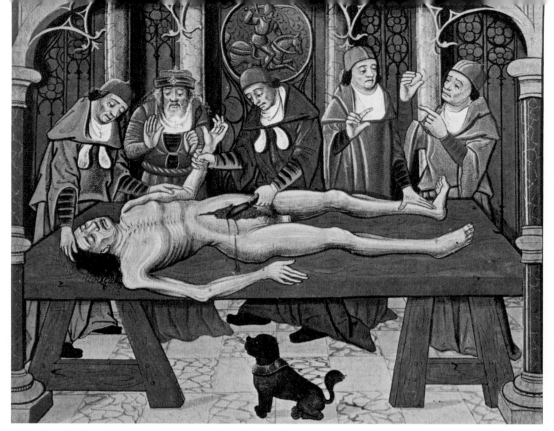

Medieval physicians dissect a body. At the time, very little was known about human physiology, and the germ theory was still unknown.

of medical knowledge and practice in medieval Europe. The concept of germs was still unknown, so people had no idea that trillions of microorganisms existed all around them (as well as on and inside their bodies). As is known today, some of these germs were harmless and some beneficial. But the more dangerous ones passed freely from person to person, from house to house, and from village to village. As a result, outbreaks of deadly diseases periodically crippled households, towns, and occasionally entire nations. Measles, leprosy, cholera, typhus, smallpox, and other debilitating maladies were rampant. And because they were ignorant of the causes

of such outbreaks, doctors could do little or nothing to stop them.

Especially calamitous was the onslaught of the bubonic plague, known as the Black Death, which struck Europe in spectacular fashion in the fourteenth century. Strains of plague were caused by a germ that infected fleas. The fleas then infested rats, a creature common in medieval society at all levels, which in turn spread the disease across the continent with alarming speed. The death toll was enormous. In a single town—Naples, Italy—some sixty-three thousand people died, and many other towns lost as many as three-quarters of their inhabitants. Modern experts estimate

Soldiers slaughter civilians in this illustration in a fifteenth-century book. Warfare was frequent, bloody, and often cruel in medieval times.

that more than 25 million people, about one-third the population of Europe, perished in only a few years.

Cruelty a Fact of Life

Catastrophic loss of life to disease played out against the backdrop of constant, grinding loss of life due to war. War is always a deadly business, and the modern age has witnessed wartime destruction on an unprecedented scale. But most modern governments and peoples generally acknowledge that war is a bad thing that should be avoided when possible, and in recent times humane rules for the treatment of prisoners, such as the Geneva Conventions, have been recognized by the international community.

In comparison, warfare in medieval Europe was brutal and cruel in the extreme, and far less romantic and chivalrous than is often depicted in modern books and films. As military historians James F. Dunnigan and Albert A. Nofi put it: "Despite the [religious warnings] against it, the Middle Ages had an enormous propensity to accept cruelty and barbarity as a fact of life."[1] Most knights and other medieval warriors fought to gain power, land, and/or money, rather than for love or honor; and many of them slaughtered their prisoners without a thought and regularly raped and murdered innocent civilians.

Thus, when considering the social status, rights, duties, and customs of various members of medieval society, one must keep in mind the world in which they lived. Their attitudes, customs, and everyday practices were in many ways shaped by the often harsh realities of that world. And those realities tended to be great levelers of rich and poor folk and of high- and low-born persons. After all, like his lowliest subjects, the loftiest king had to eat his supper by the light of candles or torches and he faced the same risk of death caused by the denizens of that microscopic realm whose existence he could not begin to imagine.

Chapter One

KINGS, VASSALS, AND SERFS: THE FEUDAL ORDER

As has been the case in all times and societies, medieval European society depended on complex networks of personal relationships. In the United States today, the predominant relationships are those between husband and wife, between parents and children, and between the individual citizen and the nation's democratic government. In medieval Europe, by contrast, the principal personal relationships were between people of lower and higher social and economic classes. People in one class or group owed allegiance and a certain set of obligations to people in a higher class, who owed similar loyalty and services to someone still higher on the social ladder. This collection of relationships has come to be known as the feudal system, or feudal order. The most powerful and prestigious figure in Europe's feudal order was the king, or chief noble of the realm; directly beneath him were the other nobles, his vassals (or retainers), who owed him allegiance. Similarly, each vassal had his own lesser retainers (or subvassals) and supporters, including soldiers, tenant farmers, and serfs.

The key to this feudal system was land, because land, rather than money, was the chief form of wealth in Europe in the Middle Ages. As one noted scholar points out:

Those who owned land [also] owned the possibility of building up military and political power, for on the land men could grow food, and men could be settled to serve and fight for their overlords. During these [medieval] centuries, free men . . . commended themselves in great numbers of their own free will to the power, service, and protection of a strong lord [who owned vast amounts of land].[2]

Ownership and exploitation of land, then, was the principal force driving the feudal system. For this reason, society became increasingly localized in character, with the great estates of kings and their leading nobles resembling chains of islands in a greater ocean of civilization called Europe. A local king, supported by

A fifteenth-century illustration fancifully depicts people from various social classes fighting one another. The rift between rich and poor was greater then than it is now.

A contemporary medieval painting of the French town of Marseilles depicts the towering stone battlements that protected both cities and castles.

his dukes, barons, counts, and other nobles, exercised commanding authority over the soldiers, farmers, tradesmen, and serfs who dwelled in his own petty kingdom. And he and the other overlords who sat at the top of the feudal pyramid erected large, well-fortified stone castles to protect their holdings and house themselves and their most important followers in safety. One of the most familiar symbols of Europe's medieval age, castles both reflected and strengthened the feudal social order that dominated that era.

Homage and Fealty

Along with the castles and landed estates that marked the physical boundaries of the feudal system, a series of solemn and dramatic ceremonies marked the differences and cemented feudal bonds between medieval European social classes. Modern society has its own symbolic social ceremonies, including the swearing-in of public officials, wedding ceremonies, oaths of citizenship, and college graduations. In medieval Europe, such ceremonies were even more important and taken very seriously. This was partly because few written contracts and records existed (since most people could not read and write) and a ceremony performed in public ensured that many witnesses could later testify that the event had in fact occurred.

Chief among the ceremonies of the feudal system was the ceremony of homage, in which a vassal lord proclaimed his allegiance to his own overlord, usually the king. The term *homage* came from the French word for man—*homme*—since the

Three young men take the oath of knighthood in the fourteenth century. Formal ceremonies and oaths were major components of Europe's feudal order.

vassal was to become the overlord's "man," in the subservient sense. The vassal clasped hands with the overlord and swore an oath of fealty, or loyalty. From that point on, the vassal owed the overlord various military and social obligations, including fighting in battle when called upon by the overlord. In return, the overlord gave the vassal either a grant of land—called a fief—or military protection, or financial support, or all of these things.

A number of eyewitness descriptions of feudal homage ceremonies have survived. The following example, which transpired in Flanders (what is now western Belgium and northern France) in the year 1127, was recorded by the medieval chronicler Galbert of Bruges. In this case, the overlord was a count named William.

They did their homage thus: The count asked if he [the vassal] was willing to become completely his man, and the other replied, "I am willing"; and with clasped hands, surrounded by the hands of the count, they were bound together by a kiss. Secondly, he who had done

Several knights swear an oath of fealty, or loyalty, to the medieval Frankish ruler Charlemagne (seated) in this fourteenth-century illustration.

homage gave his fealty to the representative of the count in these words, "I promise on my faith that I will in future be faithful to count William, and will observe my homage to him completely against all persons in good faith and without deceit," and thirdly, he took his oath to this upon the relics of the saints. [3]

Another example, an actual oath of fealty, has survived from medieval England. "I will," the vassal promises his overlord, the king,

be true and faithful, and love all which [you] love and shun all which [you] shun, according to the laws of God and the order of the world. Nor will I ever with will or action, through word or deed, do anything which is unpleasing to [you], on condition that you will hold to me as I shall deserve it, and that [you] will perform everything as it was in our agreement when I submitted myself to you. [4]

Once he had submitted to his superior lord and promised him eternal loyalty, the vassal was obliged to keep up his end of the deal. His obligations to the lord might include supplying money or other valuables to cover any shortfalls the overlord might experience. Or the overlord might call on the vassal to perform various favors, such as going on a diplomatic mission or helping the overlord find a suitable bride of high social station. Most often, however, the vassal's obligations were military in nature. Following is a feudal summons for military service issued in 1072 by King William I (best known as William the Conqueror) to one of his vassals:

William, king of the English, to Aethelwig, abbot of Evesham, greetings. I command you to summon all those who are under your charge and administration that they shall have ready before me at Clarendon . . . all the knights that they owe me. Come to me likewise yourself on that day, and bring ready with you those five knights that you owe me from your abbey. [5]

Granting a Fief

Of course, the king or other feudal overlord who had received the fealty of a vassal was also expected to keep his own end of the deal, which most often involved granting a fief. By far the most common form of fief was an estate, or manor, which usually included a house, or perhaps a small castle, plus resident peasants to work the fields. (The new owner did not own the peasants, but he did own the land they tilled and their houses, so they were beholden to him.) In the year 1200, for example, a French count named Thiebault granted one of his vassals a fief. The official document they signed reads in part:

I, Thiebault, count . . . of Troyes, make known to those present and to come that I have given in fee to Jocelyn d'Avalon and his heirs the manor which is called Gillencourt . . . and whatever [buildings, crops, tools, and so on] the same Jocelyn shall be able to acquire in the same manor I have granted to him and his heirs in augmentation of that fief.[6]

A fifteenth-century English manuscript depicts William the Conqueror, the first Norman king of England, granting land to one of his knights.

The size of fiefs varied. Some consisted of only a few acres, while others covered thousands of acres and included expanses of fertile farmland. Obviously, the vassals the king or other overlord deemed most important got the largest and most productive tracts of land.

Not all feudal fiefs consisted of land grants, however. If he felt the situation warranted it, a king or other overlord might give his vassal a sum of money and call it a fief. Other forms of fiefs included making the vassal the mayor of a town or the steward of a large estate owned by another vassal (or the steward of the king's personal lands, called the demesne). Just as there was a traditional ceremony for the act of fealty, the overlord and vassal performed one for the granting of a fief. This ceremony was called investiture because the overlord "invested," or gave authority to, the vassal.

The Manor House

In a common scenario, the new vassal received a fief consisting of an estate with a large manor house or small castle. In some cases, especially in medieval England and France, a vassal's castle was comparable in size and quality to that of his overlord. Kings usually claimed (or built) the largest and most splendid castles for themselves, but it was not unusual for some barons, dukes, or other noble vassals to live as well as their royal masters.

Whether it belonged to the king or one of his chief retainers, a medieval European castle was the central focus of life

The great hall of Hedingham Castle, in Essex, England, features an arch spanning twenty-eight feet. In this room, meetings, ceremonies, and banquets took place.

and activity on a typical feudal manor. Inside the castle or manor house, the principal room was the great hall, though it was more often called simply "the hall." (Sometimes people referred to the entire castle or house as a hall.) In the earliest castles, the great hall consisted of a very large chamber with a high ceiling. It contained numerous tables, chairs, and benches, which the servants rearranged as need dictated, as well as tapestries on the walls (partly for decoration, but also to help keep the room warm). The lord of the castle used the hall to transact busi-

ness, receive guests, and host banquets. In many cases, the hall also doubled as a sort of all-purpose lounging area, where the lord's uncles, cousins, and some of his most loyal retainers slept, ate, and socialized. Later, more sophisticated castles had a more complex great hall that often featured one or more extra stories and chambers located above the main room.

The lord himself and his wife and children slept in separate chambers located in a different part of the residence. There was also a kitchen with food pantries attached, as well as a chapel in which to

Servants scurry to and fro, waiting on the lady of a medieval French manor and her guests. The largest manors had staffs featuring dozens of servants.

pray and meditate, small chambers to house the family's servants, storerooms, and stables and other outbuildings adjoining the main house. In the early twelfth century, a French writer named Lambert of Ardres penned this description of a fairly typical manor house of the time:

The first story was on the ground level, where there were cellars and granaries and great boxes, barrels, casks, and other household utensils. In the story above were the dwelling and common rooms of the residents, including the larders [food storage], pantry [bread room] and buttery [service area for wine and beer] and the great chamber in which the lord and lady slept. Adjoining this was ... the dormitory of the ladies in waiting and the children. ... In the upper story of the house were attic rooms in which on the one side the sons of the lord of the house, when they so desired, and on the other side the daughters, because they were obliged, were accustomed to sleep. In this story also the watchmen and the servants appointed to keep the house slept at various times. High up on the east side of the house, in a convenient place, was the chapel. ... There were stairs and passages from story to story ... from room to room, and from the house into the gallery, where they used to entertain themselves with conversation, and again from the gallery into the chapel.[7]

A Manor's Outbuildings

A feudal manor house or castle such as the one Lambert describes was surrounded by smaller structures used by the servants, farmers, and laborers who maintained the estate and did all the menial work. A surviving thirteenth-century document describes some of the buildings immediately joining the main house on an estate in southern England:

Outside of [the] gate are an old house for the servants, a good stable ... and to the east of the principal building, beyond the smaller stable

An English Country Manor

Throughout most of Europe's medieval era, the lives of the rich and poor contrasted sharply. The great difference is well illustrated in a comparison of the homes of the peasants and the nobles. Most peasants lived in tiny shacks with thatched roofs and dirt floors, while their lords dwelled in magnificent stone manor houses. The following description of an English nobleman's country manor in the year 1397 comes from a surviving local public record of the period:

Extent of the manor of Keevil in the county of Wiltshire, which was [the property] of the Earl of Arundel: Within that manor are a certain hall, a chief chamber, and a little chamber next [to it] with a certain latrine [toilet room] at the back of the same hall, roofed with tiles ... a certain chapel and a cellar below the chapel ... a certain chamber called "le warderobe" likewise at the end of the hall, and the entrance thereof is a certain great chamber with a latrine, and below that chamber is a certain pantry and buttery. There is a great kitchen newly repaired.

Miscellaneous Inquisition, quoted in Clair C. Olson and Martin M. Chew, eds. *Chaucer's World.* New York: Columbia University Press, 1948, p. 331.

The laborers who worked on medieval manors performed all kinds of jobs, including felling trees, building and mending fences, and digging ditches.

... two barns, one for wheat and one for oats. These buildings are enclosed with a moat, a wall, and a hedge. Also beyond the middle gate is a good barn, and a stable of cows and another for oxen. . . . Also beyond the outer gate is a pigsty.[8]

Beyond these "outbuildings" were fields for crops, orchards, vineyards, pastures for cattle and sheep, and small farmers' huts that were sometimes grouped in tiny villages.

Manorial Workers

Most of the people who used and maintained these outbuildings, fields, pastures, and huts were rural peasants, who made up the bulk of the population of medieval Europe. Their relationship with the lord of the manor (whether a king or a vassal), their obligations to him, and the work they did for him were all parts of what over time came to be known as the manorial system (after the term *manor*). The manorial system propped up and basically made possible the feudal system because the wealthy kings and their well-to-do vassal lords could not have maintained their estates and fiefs without large numbers of cheap, loyal laborers. Without the manorial peasants to grow and harvest the crops, build and maintain the castles, and fight as foot soldiers in the wars waged by the nobles, the feudal system would have collapsed.

The workers in the manorial system owed allegiance and set obligations to their local lord, just as he owed allegiance and mandatory services to the king or other overlord. In exchange for the local lord's protection, a group of peasants agreed to perform agricultural work or some other form of labor for him for life. Most of the agricultural laborers were serfs, poor workers who were tied to the landed estate on which they toiled. In theory, they were free to leave and try to find work somewhere else. But the reality was that if they did leave, they lost a way to feed themselves and gave up their lord's military and legal protection, as well as the right to draw water from his springs and wells and to gather wood from his forests. Moreover, in an age of poor communication and transportation, there were no guarantees that better work or living conditions were available somewhere else. So most laborers stayed; they and their children, and their children's children, remained dependent manorial workers generation after generation.

These serfs, also called villeins, led difficult and usually monotonous lives. In the fall they planted wheat and rye, in the spring they sowed other grains and various vegetables, and generally in the summer they harvested the crops. The serfs also raised, fed, and when necessary slaughtered the livestock owned by the lord of the manor. They kept some of the food they produced for themselves, but a hefty share automatically went to the lord and his knights or other subvassals.

Some idea of the duties and obligations of such manorial peasants is contained in a passage from a census taken of manors and their workers in an English district in 1279. The document even preserves the man's name:

Hugh Miller holds 1 virgate [about 30 acres, or 12 ha] of land in villenage [i.e., serfdom]. . . . Hugh works through the whole year except 1 week at Christmas, 1 week at Easter [and a few other days]. . . . He gives 1 bushel of wheat . . . and 18 sheaves of oats . . . [to his lord]. Likewise he gives 3 hens and 1 cock yearly and 5 eggs at Easter. If he sells a

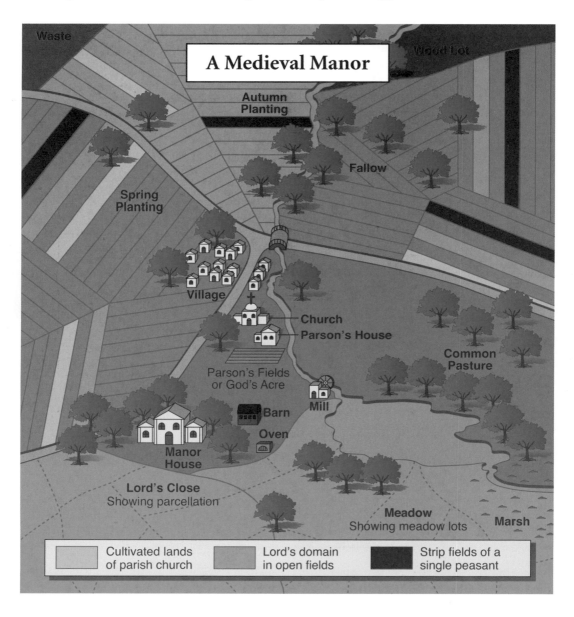

A Medieval Manor

Waste

Wood Lot

Autumn Planting

Fallow

Spring Planting

Village

Church

Parson's House

Parson's Fields or God's Acre

Common Pasture

Mill

Barn

Oven

Manor House

Lord's Close
Showing parcellation

Meadow
Showing meadow lots

Marsh

	Cultivated lands of parish church		Lord's domain in open fields		Strip fields of a single peasant

"It Is Very Hard Work"

The relentless labors medieval European serfs endured, often for very minimal rewards, are revealed in this dialogue between the early English writer Aelfric the Grammarian and a serf:

"Well, plowman, how do you work?" "Oh, Sir, I work very hard. I go out at dawn, driving the oxen to the field and I yoke them to the plow. . . . Every day I must plow a full acre or more. . . ." "Have you any mate [helper]?" "I have a boy, who drives the oxen. . . . He is now hoarse from cold and shouting [at the oxen]." "Well, is it very hard work?" "Yes indeed, it is very hard work."

Aelfric the Grammarian, *Colloquium,* quoted in Anne Fremantle and the Editors of Time Life Books, *Age of Faith.* New York: Time, 1965, p. 16.

brood mare in his courtyard for 10 [shillings] or more, he shall give [a share of the money to his lord].[9]

When workers like Hugh Miller were not busy tending to crops and livestock, they performed numerous lesser but equally demanding chores relating to the maintenance of the manor and manor house.

The Feudal Pyramid

Both the vassals of the noble class and the peasants making up the lowest classes were dependent upon and owed obligations to someone having higher status than themselves. The nobles looked to the king for protection and land grants and gave him loyalty and military service in return. Meanwhile, the workers depended on their vassal lord for jobs and security and in return maintained his estate and kept him supplied with food and other products. The single greatest beneficiary of the system was the king. Occupying the top of the feudal pyramid, he demanded and received goods and services from nearly everyone, rich and poor, and that is one reason he was able to maintain both great power and a comfortable lifestyle.

Chapter Two

SOLDIERS: RISKING AND LOSING LIFE AND LIMB

One of the most important elements of the feudal order in medieval Europe was the military service owed by a vassal lord to a king, or by various kinds of soldiers to their local lord. The vassal's commitment to fight was a common obligation and basic part of the oath of fealty he took, swearing allegiance to his king or other superior lord.

When the overlord decided to raise an army, he issued an announcement, called a summons, to the local vassal lords, who prepared themselves for war and issued their own military summons to their retainers and other men who lived and worked on their estates. These subvassals and other followers accordingly gathered their weapons and whatever armor they might own. Then the vassal lord and his men marched off to join the king's army.

That army comprised a number of different kinds of fighters who fell into two broad categories. The first and more prestigious group was made up of knights, elite soldiers who usually fought on horseback. They were elite because they were well-to-do and, with few exceptions, of high social rank. The vassal lords themselves were the chief knights of the realm, for example, and other knights were leading retainers of a vassal lord, men who lived in his castle or to whom he had granted small estates of their own. Knights had to be financially well-off, partly because horses were very expensive to breed and raise. Equipping and training a mounted warrior was also costly and time-consuming, not something a laborer busy in his fields could afford.

The second broad category of medieval fighters consisted of foot soldiers, or infantrymen. Most of these soldiers were men of lower social status than knights. Some were farmers or other peasants who worked on the king's estates or on the estates of his vassals. As a rule, the foot soldiers were not as well armored as the knights, and many infantrymen had little or no military training. Still, when used together wisely by a talented commander, an integrated army of mounted knights and foot soldiers could be highly effective on the battlefield.

Knights Idolized in Ceremony and Song

The knights who answered a king's military summons were what might be termed the rock stars of their society. Not only were they financially well-off and enjoyed high social status, they lived in or around castles, the hubs of medieval life, and people of all social classes viewed them as formidable, honorable, and at times even heroic. Knights were

A fourteenth-century manuscript shows knights leaving a castle. In medieval Europe, knights were widely respected and at times even feared.

frequently part of the splendid ceremonies held in the royal courts, and they clashed with one another in colorful tournaments, mock battles staged by kings and other nobles. "Prizes were generally offered," noted scholar Marc Bloch writes, in what became

> a distinctive class amusement, which the nobility found more exciting than any other. These meetings . . . could not be organized without consider-

able expense, [so they] usually took place on the occasion of the great "courts" held from time to time by kings or barons. Enthusiasts [of the sport] roamed the world from tournament to tournament. These were not only [ordinary] knights . . . but also very great lords. . . . Wounds were not uncommon, nor even mortal blows, when—to borrow the words of the poet Raoul de Cambrai—the jousting "took an ill turn."[10]

Two knights joust with each other in a tournament held in France in 1470. The object was to use a long lance to knock an opponent off his horse.

A man becomes a knight in an elaborate dubbing ceremony in France in the early 1500s. Typically, clergymen said prayers over the knight's sword.

Knights were also idolized and sought after by upper-class ladies, and troubadours (wandering singers) composed songs about these elite fighters. One minstrel sang:

It gives me great joy to see, drawn up on the field, knights and horses in battle array. . . . And my heart is filled with gladness when I see strong castles besieged [by these knights]. . . . And when the battle is joined, let all men of good lineage think of nothing else but the breaking of heads and arms; for it is better to die than be vanquished and live.[11]

Part of what made knights so appealing and widely respected was that they took a solemn oath to the king or a vassal lord to defend him with their lives. This act was seen as both courageous and chivalrous. Knights also took part in a special ceremony in which their superior lord "dubbed" them, or granted them the high status of knighthood. These ceremonies gained in complexity and grandeur over time, and by the twelfth and thirteenth centuries they had become major social events involving not only the nobles but also leading churchmen, who blessed the knights and their weapons.

Such ceremonies varied somewhat from place to place and time to time, but it was fairly typical for the candidate for knighthood to hand his sword to a priest, who placed the weapon on an altar and recited a prayer over it. It was also common for the holy man to call on the young man to be good of heart and use his sword only in just causes sanctioned by God. The candidate also emphasized his respect for God by cutting his hair short, in the style worn by monks. Sometimes the knight-to-be underwent a ritual bath to symbolize his purification before the king and God. Then he donned special robes, shoes, and a helmet. During the ceremony, his king, duke, or other overlord presented him with a spur to wear in battle and a new, ornately decorated sword. The overlord then recited words to this effect: "Knight, God grant you a life of honor, that you may be a man of great trust and worth, in thought, word, and deed."[12]

Obligations of Knights

Once a man became a knight, he was bound to fulfill set obligations to his overlord. These included not only military service in wartime, but also certain duties in peacetime. For example, if the king was not waging war, it was common for a knight to serve a given number of days, usually about forty, each year guarding the local castle. The following list of military rules for vassals and other knights dates from late-thirteenth-century France:

> All vassals of the king are bound to appear before him when he shall summon them, and to serve him at their own expense for forty days and forty nights, with as many knights as each one owes; and he is able to extract from them these services when he wishes and when he has need of them. And if the king wishes to keep them more than forty days at their own expense, they are not bound to remain if they do not wish it. And if the king wishes to keep them at his expense for the defense of the realm, they are bound to remain.[13]

When on duty in peacetime, knights usually lived in the castles they guarded. In the early medieval centuries, when most castles were still fairly small, they could house only a few soldiers—perhaps no more than half a dozen or so. Later, when castles grew larger, it was not unusual for as many as twenty to fifty knights to find temporary or even permanent quarters in the lord's residence.

In wartime, by contrast, a knight usually had to serve sixty or more days and to provide horses, arms, and supplies at his own expense. He was also expected to take along servants and even some of his own minor retainers, usually foot soldiers, to help and support him while on campaign. A unit made up of a knight and his retainers and other followers was called a lance. During a campaign, the members of a lance most often lodged in tents.

A Remedy for Boredom?

Marc Bloch, a noted scholar of the feudal order, suggests that medieval knights might have been willing to take up arms and fight for their lords in part because their private, privileged lives were otherwise simply boring and bred restlessness.

Accustomed to danger, the knight found in war yet another attraction. It offered a remedy for boredom. For these men . . . were seldom occupied by very heavy administrative cares, [and] everyday life easily slipped into a gray monotony. Thus was born an appetite for diversions [such as fighting] in distant lands. William the Conqueror . . . said of one of his vassals . . . "I do not think it would be possible to find a better knight in arms; but he is unstable . . . and spends his time gadding about from place to place."

Marc Bloch, *Feudal Society*, trans. L.A. Manyon. London: Routledge, 1989, p. 295.

Knights clash in battle in fourteenth-century France. Combat was often the high point of a knight's life.

Besieging castles was a common tactic in medieval warfare. Here, soldiers use a variety of weapons, including crude firearms, against an enemy castle.

Weapons and Tactics of Knights

Modern books and films that depict knights on military campaigns usually show them wearing armor made of heavy metal plates, brandishing long lances, and riding horses also decked out in armor.

However, these "heavy cavalrymen" did not appear until the second half of the Middle Ages. Early medieval European knights, who followed the lead of Frankish (early French) cavalrymen, wore light armor made of mail (rows of iron rings or scales either riveted or sewn together to form a heavy protective shirt). Mail armor was fairly flexible and allowed the rider to maneuver his horse and use his weapons with greater ease than was possible for later heavy cavalrymen. The most common weapons wielded by these early knights were swords, throwing spears, and, on occasion, bows. They also sometimes carried shields.

The tactics employed by the early medieval knights also differed from those that came later. Frankish and other light cavalrymen did not engage in shock action—direct charges on either cavalry or infantry. Such charges would have caused them to fall from their mounts in the midst of battle, because these horsemen did not have the benefit of the stirrup, which helps a rider maintain his balance and position atop his horse. When stirrups began to be adopted in western Europe in the early eighth century, they made mounted warriors more formidable. Yet shock action was still seldom used in battle. The earliest knights mainly chased off ambushers, pursued fleeing enemies, raided villages, or harassed the flanks (sides) of enemy troop formations. It was also quite common for these early medieval horsemen to dismount and fight on foot alongside the infantrymen.

As time went on, however, the armor worn by knights became heavier and more protective. Starting in the eleventh

The Evolution of Armor

1200 A.D.
Early knights wore a chain mail suit covered by a cloth tunic and carried a simple spear and heavyweight shield.

1400 A.D.
Even later knights wore steel-plated full body armor that covered a chain mail suit, metal bell-shaped gauntlets (gloves) with cloth fingers, a helmet with a cut-out visor, a two-handed sword, and a knife.

1200 A.D.　　1300 A.D.　　1400 A.D.　　1500 A.D.

1300 A.D.
Later knights added a domed steel-plated helmet with rigid faceplate, a lightweight shield bearing a coat of arms, and a single-handed sword.

1500 A.D.
The latest knights of the Middle Ages had steel-plated full body armor reinforced at the knees, elbows, and feet with thick points that acted as weapons, a helmet with hinged faceplate, and a longer two-handed sword.

Many Knights Lacked Discipline

The knights making up units of heavy cavalry were well protected against the blows of enemy weapons. But their armor was very bulky and inflexible; indeed, if they fell to the ground they had trouble standing up unaided. As scholars James F. Dunnigan and Albert A. Nofi explain, their performance in battle was also hindered by a less tangible disadvantage—their conceited attitude.

The basic problem was that every noble (knights and above in social rank) thought he was above obeying orders. A duke or a count had some control over his knights . . . but each such noble was less impressed by the royal official, or king himself, in charge of the entire army. Every noble thought he, and his troops, deserved the post of honor in the first rank. Any army commander would try to line up his various contingents in such a way that each would be used to best effect. Most knights (of whatever rank) simply wanted to get at an enemy and fight it out man to man. This was the mentality of knights through most of the medieval period.

James F. Dunnigan and Albert A. Nofi, "Medieval Warfare," in *Medieval Life & the Hundred Years War.* www.hyw.com/books/history/Medi0000.htm.

century, mail shirts became longer and heavier and sometimes stretched to the knees. A coif, a mail hood that covered the head, also became common attire for knights. Then mail arm and leg coverings, as well as mail gloves, were added, and by about 1250 many knights wore metal plates over the mail on their knees, elbows, and other joints. The natural culmination of this trend was full plate armor, as well as armor for the horses.

Although these heavy cavalrymen were much better protected than earlier knights, their massive suits of armor limited their flexibility. So they could no longer employ the fairly wide array of weapons wielded by early medieval cavalry. The spear and bow were abandoned, and the main weapon was now the sword. The lance, often used in tournament displays, was also introduced into battle. The key to the effectiveness of the lance was the ability of the horseman to absorb a great deal of shock and stay mounted when the weapon hit an opponent. The stirrup provided some stability, but not until the introduction of larger, wraparound saddles did cavalry charges with leveled lances become an effective offensive tactic.

The heavily armored knights who fought during the 1200s, 1300s, and 1400s in Europe were often highly lethal, especially when used in concert with infantry. But there was always the danger of the knights losing their effectiveness if they became overconfident. Because they were almost always part of the social elite in their native realms, knights were often proud, vain, and arrogant. This could lead to disaster. One of the classic examples took place in the year 1119 when Louis VI, king of France, led a force of some four hundred knights into English-controlled Normandy (in northwestern France). There he faced off with the English king Henry I, who commanded five hundred knights. Henry ordered four hundred of his horsemen to dismount and form an armored wall of heavy infantry behind the other hundred, who remained mounted. Then Louis unwisely ordered all of his men to lower their lances and charge the enemy. His knights managed to break through the smaller force of English horsemen, but just as Henry had anticipated, this slowed the French charge almost to a halt. Protected by their heavy armor, the English knights who had dismounted swarmed around the French riders, pulling them from their horses and either killing or capturing them.

Raising Units of Foot Soldiers

This small-scale battle between Louis and Henry demonstrated the importance of foot soldiers on the battlefield. Infantry

Foot soldiers grapple with one another in this medieval illustration. Most foot soldiers lived and worked in villages or on manors when they were not fighting.

Foot Soldiers' Bows of Choice

The English longbow and the crossbow were favorite weapons of many European foot soldiers. Sidney Toy, an expert on medieval warfare, describes the advantages of each kind of bow.

The crossbow was in general use by the end of the twelfth century and, except among the English, was the favorite [hand] weapon from that time to the latter part of the fifteenth century. In open warfare the English preferred the longbow, which was about 6 ft. long. The longbow was light while the crossbow was heavy and cumbersome. With the longbow the archer could shoot about five arrows while the crossbow was discharging one bolt, and he could keep his eye on the foe during the adjustment of a new missile, while the crossbowman's whole attention was required for this purpose. In the defense of fortifications, however . . . the crossbow, with its heavier missile, greater force, and longer range was by far the superior weapon.

Sidney Toy, *Castles: Their Construction and History*. New York: Dover, 1985, pp. 141–42.

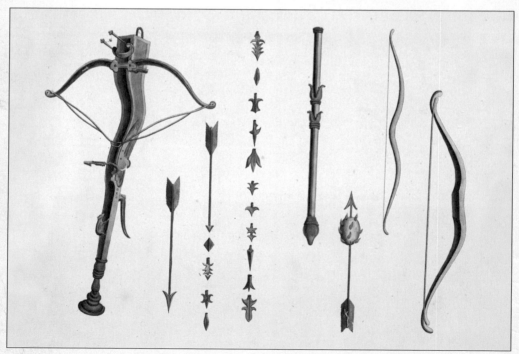

A collection of common medieval arms includes a crossbow (left), two simple bows (right), and various arrows and other missiles.

An illustration dating from the fifteenth century shows a battle fought among foot soldiers near a fortified French town.

could be used in conjunction with cavalrymen, as happened often in wars in the Middle Ages. Or foot soldiers could be deployed on their own, to overrun villages, for instance, or to seize castles and fortified cities. These fighters were most often divided into two broad groups—those who could afford weapons and did the bulk of the fighting, and the very poor, who did menial labor. The latter generally carried equipment, set up military camps, dug trenches, and so forth. Very

little is known about these laborers, since contemporary accounts were written by upper-class men who held the peasants in contempt and largely ignored them.

However, a fair amount is known about the foot soldiers who actually fought in battles and attacked fortifications. Like the vassals and knights who swore allegiance to the kings, the lowlier foot soldiers were products of the feudal and manorial systems. Most infantrymen were, like knights, part-time soldiers.

Some lived in cities, where they might work as laborers or artisans. But larger numbers of potential infantrymen dwelled in the countryside on manors, where they tilled the soil, raised animals, or performed other menial jobs. When a king, baron, or other nobleman needed to raise a force of foot soldiers, he called on his vassals to supply him with men. The farmers, workers, or other men called up for service were expected to grab whatever weapons they could find and assemble in a predetermined place, ready to march off to war. Under the feudal system in most parts of Europe, each manor was expected to supply a certain number of foot soldiers; they made up a unit known as a retinue.

In most cases, the number of infantrymen in a retinue was a good deal larger than the number of knights and other men in a lance. In the 1300s, for example, an English noble, Richard Lord Talbot, had a retinue that included eighty-two archers and sixty other soldiers, whereas he was able to field only fourteen knights. Like knights, most foot soldiers were obliged to serve for forty days. If a campaign lasted longer, they might stay on. But this was the exception rather than rule, partly because these men were also needed to maintain the crops of and perform other essential duties on the manors, and if large numbers of them were gone too long, food shortages and other problems could ensue.

Thus, kings and other nobles who tried to raise armies in medieval Europe often found that candidates for the infantry were limited in number at any given time. Also, even when enough men could be found, many of them were often not up to the task. For one thing, most lacked any sort of military training or experience. Even worse, large numbers of these men were inadequately equipped, having little or no armor and few effective weapons. Some actually marched off to battle carrying pitchforks and other farm implements. For these reasons, it was fairly common practice for feudal lords to supplement their locally raised foot soldiers with foreign mercenaries, professional soldiers who hired themselves out to anyone willing to pay their price. Mercenaries were generally very well armed, well trained, and battle hardened, and they usually served for as long as they were needed. So having a hard core of them in an army gave a king or other commander definite military advantages.

Weapons and Tactics of Foot Soldiers

Whether they were peasants called into service or mercenaries paid to fight, medieval foot soldiers used a fairly wide variety of weapons. Some were more prevalent in certain parts of Europe than others, and choices of weapons could vary from era to era. Moreover, even in a given place and time, there was usually not much uniformity. This was because foot soldiers were mostly men of modest means and used whatever weapons they could afford or were most readily available. In general, the weapons included swords, daggers (frequently used to cut the throats of knights who had fallen from their mounts), spears and pikes (very long spears), axes (favored by the Vikings and Germans, though used by others as well), maces (clubs), standard bows and cross-bows (which came into wide use in Europe in the twelfth century), and crude handguns (which appeared in the last few medieval centuries). Shields of differing sizes and shapes were also employed.

The ways these weapons were used on the battlefield also varied widely. Some countries and peoples specialized in or emphasized one or more weapons; for example, the English long relied on infantrymen armed with deadly longbows that unleashed vast swarms of arrows onto enemy lines, doing tremendous damage. Foot soldiers wielding swords and daggers, aided by cavalry, then followed up. In contrast, the Scots and Swiss

Most medieval battles featured many different kinds of soldiers wielding a wide variety of weapons. There was no typical medieval soldier.

Medieval Weapons

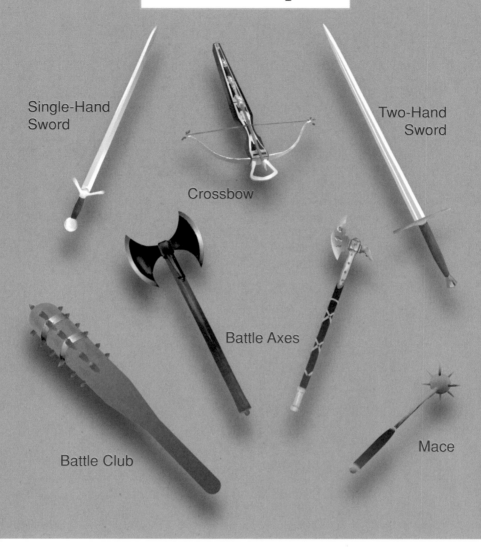

Single-Hand Sword

Two-Hand Sword

Crossbow

Battle Axes

Battle Club

Mace

developed tightly packed formations of foot soldiers holding long pikes. These formations, called phalanxes, resembled giant porcupines with their quills erect, and when they moved forward the enemy more often than not gave way.

Thus, Europe's feudal and manorial systems produced a staggeringly diverse array of fighting men having highly var-ied backgrounds and wielding many different kinds of weapons. In short, there was no standard or typical medieval warrior. All of them (except foreign mercenaries) had one thing in common, though. They followed orders and fought because the traditions and rules of the feudal order, which governed their society, obliged them to do so.

Chapter Three

PEOPLE OF FAITH: HEARTS AND MINDS DEVOTED TO GOD

More than any other single force, the Christian church shaped the thought and behavior of medieval Europeans. Indeed, the church and its numerous representatives— collectively called the clergy—exerted a profoundly strong grip on society as a whole and served as a unifying force for European civilization. This influence was in large part a result of the disintegration of the mighty Roman Empire in the fifth and sixth centuries. The Roman Empire had long controlled the Mediterranean region and many other parts of Europe, and its fall left a major political and cultural vacuum. In many areas there was little or no centralized authority. So for fellowship and mutual protection people tended to huddle together in small villages and on farms. Most people were poor peasants who had no time for learning, reading, or cultural or spiritual pursuits. Even the handful of local nobles who came to rule each local region were largely lacking in culture and religious training.

Like people in all times and places, both the poor and the well-off yearned for solace and direction in their lives. So they readily sought out those few people who were educated and seemed to have spiritual connections with God. In most cases, clergymen were by far the most educated people around, more learned than many kings and nobles. Thus, even society's most powerful individuals came to rely on the clergy for wide-ranging advice, sometimes even in political and diplomatic decisions. The "neglect of education among the laity [ordinary people]," Bloch remarks, "explains the role of the clergy both as interpreters of the ideas of the great [kings and lords] and as [shapers] of political tradition." [14]

A worshiper (left) places some valuables in a bag after a church service. Such offerings helped to support the clergymen who ran the churches.

Members of the clergy thus became the spiritual and often the intellectual and social guides for most Europeans. Clergymen of one kind or another were everywhere, and people respected, consulted, resisted, loved, feared, appeased, or joined them, depending on the time, place, and situation. Churchmen also wisely and effectively increased their influence at all levels of society by making themselves an integral part of the feudal order. As former University of Delaware scholar Walther Kirchner puts it:

> Church authorities voluntarily assumed some of the feudal obligations of a landholder. They paid their overlord with some of the food grown on the land. . . . Sometimes they would go so far as to send peasants and knights inhabiting church lands to serve in the military forces of kings and lords. Such a situation necessarily led to a further involvement of the church in feudal affairs. Consequently, those lords who depended upon church support became more and more eager to influence the appointment of bishops . . . and even ordinary priests.[15]

Priests and Monks

Two distinct branches of the clergy evolved in medieval Europe. The first was the ordinary priesthood, or secular clergy, consisting of parish priests, bishops, and other official representatives of the main Christian church in Rome. These clergymen provided ordinary people with religious ceremonies, sermons, and sacraments such as Holy Communion, baptism, and marriage.

The other branch of the clergy was the so-called regular clergy, made up of monks. These godly folk took vows of poverty, chastity, and obedience and spent most of their time praying and meditating in secluded monasteries; therefore, the groups, or orders, to which they belonged were part of what came to be called the monastic movement.

The first major and widely influential medieval monastic order was that of the Benedictines, founded by Saint Benedict in the sixth century. Benedict was born a Roman aristocrat and grew up in Italy in the late fifth century. Shortly after the year 500, he decided to withdraw from worldly life, began to gather a number of dedicated followers, and in 529 established a monastery at Monte Cassino, situated in the hills between Rome and Naples. Much of Benedict's importance to the medieval world stemmed from the fact that he dutifully wrote down the tenets and routines he had developed for his monastic retreat. This document is titled *The Rule*. It became, in a real sense, the blueprint for hundreds of monasteries established across Europe in the following centuries. Scholar Paul Johnson summarizes some of the main routines the Benedictines and many other monks followed:

> Monks were to have separate beds, except the younger ones, who were to be "dispersed among the seniors."

Benedict Disdains Idleness

In this brief passage from his treatise titled The Rule, *Benedict, founder of the Benedictine Order, stresses the importance of remaining busy and productive at all times.*

Idleness is the enemy of the soul. The brethren [i.e., the monks living in the monastery], therefore, must be occupied at stated hours in manual labor, and again at other hours in sacred reading. To this end, we think that the times for each may be determined in the following manner. From Easter until September the 14th, the brethren shall start work in the morning and from the first hour until the fourth do the tasks that have to be done. From the fourth hour until about the sixth, let them apply themselves to reading. After the sixth hour, having left the [dinner] table, let them rest on their beds in perfect silence; or if anyone wishes to read by himself, let him read so as not to disturb the others.

Saint Benedict, Abbot of Monte Cassino, *The Rule of St. Benedict,* trans. Justin McCann. London: Burns, Oates, and Washbourne, 1952, p. 42.

A painting dating from the early 1400s depicts Saint Benedict presenting a copy of The Rule *to the monks of Monte Cassino in Italy.*

They were to be properly and warmly clad, with two tunics and cowls each; and they were issued with a mattress, a woolen blanket . . . and pillow, shoes, stockings . . . knife, pen and writing tablets, needle and handkerchiefs. Otherwise, no property was to be held individually. . . . Monks were to be adequately but simply fed: two cooked dishes a day, a pound of bread, a pint of wine, and fruit and vegetables in season, but no meat, at any rate of four-footed beasts. . . . The monks were to spend their time in manual labor and sacred reading, when not attending divine services. They were to practice "silence at all times, especially during the night." [16]

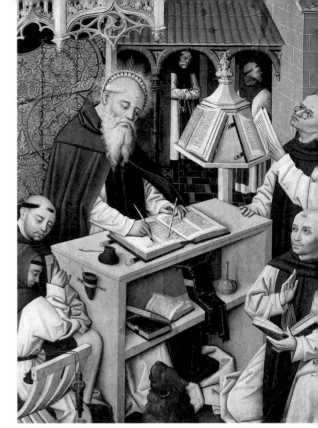

A late medieval painting shows a group of industrious monks copying and studying manuscripts.

Partly because they spent so much time reading and studying, many monks were extremely well read as well as talented scholars, musicians, and artisans. They shared their knowledge with other monks, and in some cases they established schools on the grounds of the monasteries, which over time gained reputations as relatively safe places in times of war or plague. In this way the medieval clergy steadily became a repository of knowledge in history, literature, music, art, and other disciplines.

Such well-educated and versatile clergymen are well illustrated by three monks who lived in the abbey at Saint Gall, in Switzerland, in the ninth century. Their story was told by a local scholar and chronicler named Ekkehard, who also

hailed from Saint Gall. The priest named Notker, he said, "was frail in body," but "not in spirit." He was "lofty in divine thoughts, patient in adversity," and very skilled "in illuminating [illustrating manuscripts], reading and composing." In comparison, the second priest, Tutilo, was "strong and supple in arm and limb." Tutilo was also "clear of voice, a delicate carver and painter," and "musical, with especial skill on the harp and the flute." As for the third priest, Ratpert, Ekkehard wrote that he was a "master of schools," who was "a straightforward and kindly teacher." [17]

Disharmony in the Clerical Ranks

In general the secular clergy looked after people's everyday spiritual needs, while the monastic orders set an example of holiness for others to follow and promoted learning and the preservation of knowledge. One might assume that the two kinds of clergy would get along and actively support each other; after all, they were all Christians and avowed followers of the one Christian church, based in Rome. However, the reality was that rivalries and mutual contempt among priests and monks became fairly common in medieval Europe.

One bone of contention among the two clerical groups was the tithe, or church tax. This mandatory church fee most often consisted of 10 percent of a person's income and applied to all members of a parish. In addition to collecting their parishioners' tithes, priests also charged fees for the various services they performed, and some quietly pocketed part of the considerable funds the church collected for charity. Thus, a number of priests, especially bishops and other high church officials, became rich and enjoyed luxuries and a standard of living comparable to those of many nobles. Not surprisingly, the monastic orders, whose members had taken strict vows of poverty, objected to these practices. It was not unusual for monks to look on the majority of priests as corrupt and badly in need of spiritual reform.

Strong disagreements and rivalries also existed between the monks and friars, whose orders were an offshoot of the monastic movement. In the early 1200s, Saint Dominic, who preached in Spain and southern France, and Saint Francis of Assisi, who preached in Italy, both objected strongly to the idea of clergymen withdrawing from the regular world. In their view, this went against Christ's order to his disciples to go out into the world and urge people to repent and follow God. So Dominic established a new order that took his name—the Dominicans—and Francis founded the Franciscan Order of friars. The members of these groups dedicated themselves not only to remaining poor, but also to performing public service. They ministered to the poorest of the poor, including beggars, and earned their food by working in farmers' fields and the workshops of merchants. Friars refused to ask for tithes and often wore old clothes that other people had discarded. Monks and ordinary priests frequently saw friars as too conservative, and even as irritating extremists. But many ordinary people respected the friars for their selfless devotion to God and were eager to hear them preach.

Europe's Chief Clergyman

Whether they were parish priests, bishops, monks, or friars, all Christian clergymen professed to love God and obey his will. They also recognized, in varying degrees, the authority of the man all medieval Europeans recognized as God's chief vicar on Earth—the pope. (Bishops and priests answered directly to the pope in a standard hierarchy, or ladder of authority; monks and friars at times had less direct ties to the pope, and some ignored his edicts when they could get away with it.)

The institution of the papacy evolved slowly over time during Christianity's early centuries and did not emerge as a powerful force in Europe until the period immediately following Rome's fall. The most influential figure in defining the papacy and solidifying its authority in this era was Pope Gregory I, who was born in about

Saint Francis (right) has an audience with the pope in this fourteenth-century illustration. Francis founded the Franciscan Order of friars.

540. Gregory dispatched monks to convert the pagans (non-Christians) in England. He also established a number of standards that later medieval and modern popes would follow. At a time when Italy was threatened by barbarian tribes from the Alps and beyond, Gregory took charge of Rome and kept its inhabitants safe. This established him and his papal office as political as well as spiritual forces to be reckoned with. He also expanded the existing church bureaucracy and penned a tract titled *Pastoral Rule*, which became the standard manual of conduct for medieval bishops.

As time went on, most of Gregory's papal successors tried to promote the idea of theocracy, a system in which the church would have supreme authority over secular, or nonchurch, affairs. In theory, this would give the popes even greater authority in society than that of kings and their principal feudal vassals. The feudal kings and nobles were all Christians and accepted the church's role as a spiritual guide for society. However, these leaders were very reluctant to hand over their political sovereignty to a clergyman who had only holy words, rather than armed troops, to back up his authority. As a result, a long, on-and-off struggle ensued between the popes and secular leaders over whose authority should be higher.

This contest between church and state reached a major climax not long after the ascension of Pope Gregory VII in 1073. Gregory daringly proclaimed that Christ's church on Earth was infallible and all powerful—and anyone, even including the loftiest of kings, who openly challenged it and the edicts issued by its leaders was not a true Christian and would be rejected by God. Many European monarchs feared Gregory and the potential he had for swaying the hearts and minds of the general populace. But one king, Germany's Henry IV, defied the pope, calling him a false monk and demanding that he resign his office. "You have not won favor from the common herd [of Christian worshipers] by crushing them," Henry wrote to Gregory.

> You have looked upon all of them as knowing nothing [and] upon yourself as knowing all things.... Let another [man] ascend the throne of St. Peter, who shall ... practice the sound doctrine of St. Peter. I, Henry, king by the grace of God, do say to you ... descend to the damned [i.e., "go to hell"].[18]

In retaliation for this affront, Gregory excommunicated Henry, which supposedly denied the king the right to enter heaven and receive salvation. This act struck fear into Henry's vassals and other subjects, and most abandoned him. After holding out for only two months, he had no choice but to relent, and in an astonishing display, the greatest monarch on the continent was forced to stand barefoot in the snow for days until Gregory forgave and reinstated him.

This victory did not by any means make Gregory the ruler of all Europe. He

One of the earliest and greatest popes, Gregory I, takes part in a procession in Rome. Gregory established many standard practices for clergymen.

Gregory VII absolves King Henry IV at the conclusion of their bitter power struggle. Gregory and the papacy emerged as the clear winners.

and his successors still lacked a country and armies to back up their authority. But the confrontation between the two men established that the papacy would thereafter command a degree of respect and earthly power roughly equal to that held by an average king.

Reasons for the Clergy's Success

Within the hierarchy of the church itself, however, the pope's authority remained virtually supreme. He was the boss, so to speak, not only of the bishops, priests,

52 Lords, Ladies, Peasants, and Knights: Class in the Middle Ages

and members of the monastic orders, but also of a number of other kinds of godly people in medieval society. Among these were the deacons, nuns, and pardoners. Deacons were senior members of local parishes who helped the parsons (parish priests) maintain the churches and conduct weekly services. Nuns were members of female monastic orders. They lived and prayed in institutions called convents, or priories, each headed by a female overseer called a prioress. A pardoner was a church official who, when a priest asked him to do so, pardoned someone who had recently done some sort of penance to absolve him- or herself of sin.

Together the different kinds of clergy and other servants of God represented a significant part of the population of medieval Europe. No accurate figures for just how great a percentage that was have survived, but modern experts believe it was much higher than it is today. One indication can perhaps be inferred from *The Canterbury Tales*. Penned in the late 1300s by the English poet Geoffrey Chaucer, this great work of English literature chronicles the conversation and tales of a group of people from many walks of life who go on a pilgrimage to a major shrine in southern England. (Hundreds of thousands of medieval people in each new generation periodically made long trips to various distant churches and shrines to pray and show their devotion to God.) About a quarter of this varied group are affiliated in some way with the church (including, among others, a par-

son, a pardoner, and a prioress). Of course, it may well be that this reflects only that Chaucer was personally more interested in clergymen and other religious people than he was in ordinary people. But a number of modern scholars think it shows that clergy and other godly people must have collectively made up a fairly large proportion of the population.

The fact that so many people were members of the clergy or otherwise affiliated with the church, not to mention the large numbers of ordinary people who went on

The first page of an original manuscript of Chaucer's Canterbury Tales.

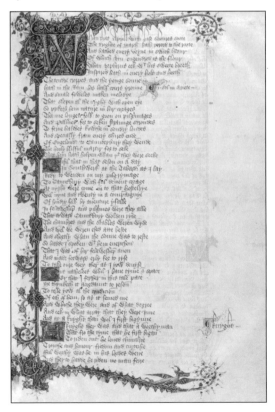

Proving the Existence of God

In his great work the Summa Theologica, *Thomas Aquinas gave five arguments that he felt proved the existence of God. Brief excerpts from two of these arguments are presented here.*

The existence of God can be proven in five ways. The first ... is the argument from motion. It is ... evident from our senses that some things [in the universe, such as the Sun and moon] are in motion. ... Whatever is in motion must be put in motion by another. ... And this [mover] everyone understands to be God. The second way is from ... causation. ... There is no case known ... in which a thing is found to be the ... cause of itself. ... Therefore, it is necessary to put forward a first cause, to which everyone gives the name of God.

Thomas Aquinas, *Summa Theologica,* trans. Fathers of the English Dominican Province. New York: Benziger Brothers, 1911, pp. 19–20.

A painting dating from ca. 1500 shows members of the Dominican Order accepting Thomas Aquinas into their number.

such religious pilgrimages, demonstrates the extensive influence religion held over people's minds and lives. Churchmen were successful in imposing their will and religious rules on the masses partly because they could, when need dictated, instill real fear in the members of their flocks. Clear-ly, few people were willing to risk, as King Henry had, the prospect of excommunica-tion and eternal damnation.

On a gentler, more positive note, however, priests and other clergymen also regularly won people's hearts and minds by enlightening them about God. In both formal sermons and informal conversations, they explained God's nature, what he expected of human beings, and the benefits of adhering to the rules God had supposedly set down in the Bible.

For those few who doubted the existence of God, some leading clergymen developed what seemed to them reasoned proofs that such a deity was in fact very real. The culmination of such arguments was that composed by theologian Thomas Aquinas, one of the greatest scholars of the Middle Ages. In his masterwork, the *Summa Theologica,* he attempted to systematically present all of Christian theology as logically as possible, refuting arguments he believed were incorrect and offering reasoned "proof," for example, of the existence of God.

This intellectual movement, called medieval scholasticism, carried much weight and was very compelling to the inhabitants of medieval Europe, educated and uneducated alike. The *Summa Theologica* and other writings by medieval clergymen and religious thinkers helped to shape the intellectual atmosphere of the Middle Ages. In so doing, they ensured that Christianity and its spokesmen at all levels of society would long remain Europe's spiritual guides. It is no wonder that medieval times have so often been called "the age of faith."

Chapter Four

WOMEN: DOING THEIR DUTIES IN A MAN'S WORLD

In any discussion of medieval Europe and the feudal system that largely determined its political and social structure, it is difficult to avoid using male-specific terms. After all, almost all political, social, and religious authority figures were men. Kings, barons, dukes, vassals, knights, town councilmen, priests, monks, and friars were all male. Exceptions—that is, women with any sort of authority—included the prioresses of convents and an occasional queen who held power and influence in the royal court. But a prioress's authority was strictly limited to the convent itself, and she could be overruled by her male superiors in the church hierarchy. As for those few queens who briefly sat on thrones after their husbands died, in the words of scholar Pauline Stafford, "none of these women ruled in their own right, as a female king. Nor was their position as

secure as that of a male ruler."[19] (In the military realm, the famous case of the French maiden Joan of Arc, who led armies of men in battle, is a unique, and uniquely famous, exception.) Clearly, medieval Europe was, for the most part, a man's world.

Yet women did make up roughly half the population of that world. And in spite of their lack of authority, society could not have functioned without them. Therefore, any balanced study of medieval society must address the status, treatment, duties, and activities of women. Their status, opportunities, and treatment varied somewhat from place to place in Europe, and especially from one social class to another. But generally speaking, the vast majority of men saw women as the inferior sex, both physically and intellectually. This view was supported and strengthened by church officials, who, of course, were all men. Bishops and priests urged women to "know their place," to obey their fathers and husbands, and to adhere to the womanly virtues and "natural" male-dominated order supposedly established by God.

A woman's "place" in medieval society depended on various factors, the most important of which were her family's social status and economic means. Women of the lower classes worked diligently, either at home or in various trades. In contrast, most upper-class women had no need to work for a living and instead pursued refined pastimes such as needlework or playing a musical instrument in the context of a life of leisure supported by well-to-do fathers or husbands. But whether rich or poor, social mores dictated that all women be soft-spoken, avoid speaking out of turn, walk in a "ladylike" manner and never run, and never embarrass their husbands or other male relatives. Most conformed to these conventions, at

A fifteenth-century French painting depicts the famous maiden Joan of Arc telling French ruler Charles VII that she has captured the city of Orleans.

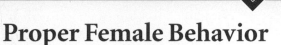

Proper Female Behavior

One of the principal social norms of Europe in the Middle Ages was that women (particularly of the upper classes) were expected to behave modestly and quietly at all times, particularly in public. This is an excerpt from Chatoiement des Dames, *a guide to proper female behavior by a popular medieval poet, Robert of Blois.*

O n the way to church or elsewhere, a lady must walk straight and not trot or run, or idle either. She must salute even the poor. She must let no one touch her on the breast except her husband. For that reason, she must not let anyone put a pin or a brooch on her bosom. No one should kiss her on the mouth except her husband. If she disobeys this injunction, neither loyalty, faith nor noble birth will avert the consequences. . . . If a man courts a lady, she must not boast of it. It is base [unseemly] to boast. . . . Women must not

swear, drink too much or eat too much. . . . Cut your fingernails frequently, down to the quick, for cleanliness' sake. Cleanliness is better than beauty.

Quoted in Joseph Gies and Frances Gies, *Life in a Medieval City.* New York: Harper & Row, 1981, pp. 56–57.

Among the tasks deemed proper for medieval women was gardening.

least publicly, but some inevitably broke them and were duly chastised.

Although most men accepted that women were inferior beings, some of the conventions of feudal chivalry seemed to contradict this notion. At the height of the Middle Ages, many upper-class men

worshiped, often in songs and poetry, an idealized image of pure, innocent, dignified womanhood. The word *idealized* is key here. This seeming contradiction in the social order was based on romantic, chivalrous ideals of female virtue and beauty. The unattainable image usually

The idealized medieval image of a dignified, saintly woman being rescued or protected by a strong man is illustrated in this fifteenth-century woodcut.

bore little relation to the circumstances of real women's lives, which were far from ideal. Thus, there existed in medieval Europe a peculiar double standard regarding women and their roles and images in society.

Some Marriages Unhappy

This double standard can be seen in the institution of marriage. Many medieval marriages were arranged by parents, guardians, or the local overlord (a king or one of his vassals). So large numbers of women had no say in who their mate would be and began their adult lives (most girls were considered adults and married at puberty, or even earlier) at the very least at an emotional disadvantage. Moreover, if the marriage was unhappy, there was often nothing the woman could do about it. The church strongly discouraged or forbade divorce. It *was* possible to get a marriage annulled, or wiped off the records as if it never happened. But this required attending a hearing with church officials, who only rarely granted such annulments. Also, men were the ones who more often managed to use this loophole to their own advantage. A man could marry a woman from a well-to-do family, for instance, and after spending most or all of her money, petition the church for an annulment on the grounds that she was actually of servile status and had tricked him into the marriage.

Society, including the church and sometimes local laws, also supported a man's right to abuse his wife physically. Indeed, wife beating was fairly common. An influential thirteenth-century Dominican monk preached that "a man may chastise [punish] his wife and beat her for correction, for she is of the household, therefore the lord [husband] may chastise his own." [20] Similarly, when the new French town of Villefranche was established in that same century, one of its laws stated: "All [male] inhabitants of Villefranche have the right to beat their wives, provided they do not kill them thereby." [21] There were no class restrictions on such abuse. Records show that one rich nobleman kicked his wife in the face, breaking her nose, and later bragged about it. Meanwhile, peasant or village women were not only punched and kicked, but were sometimes punished by "ducking." The unfortunate victim was tied to a stool and dipped repeatedly below the surface of a local pond.

Though the frequency of such punishments varied from place to place and family to family, battering women may have been fairly common among the lower classes, as evidence suggests that many peasant women were quite outspoken. Yet it is also probable that some of the more outspoken women avoided punishment: Many accounts describe women who are tough, earthy characters who dominate their timid husbands and actually make some of the more important family decisions. The most familiar example to modern audiences is Chaucer's "Wife of Bath," a colorful member of the religious pilgrimage he described in *The Canterbury Tales*. Married five times, she is not afraid to express herself openly, even about private

This illustration in a late medieval version of The Canterbury Tales *shows the Wife of Bath.*

matters that neither men nor women are supposed to talk about in public. In the mixed company of pilgrims, for example, she pointedly declares that the human genitals were made for sex as well as urination.

Exceptions to the Rule

There were exceptions to this rule of abusive marital relationships, of course. Surviving evidence indicates that some men loved their wives deeply and treated them with gentleness, kindness, and respect. An outstanding example was Thomas Betson, a forty-year-old English merchant, who wrote to his fiancée (and cousin) in 1476:

My own heartily beloved Cousin Katherine, I recommend me to you with all the inwardness of my heart. . . . I received a token from you, [which] is to me right heartily welcome and with glad will I received it. . . . I understand right well that you be in good health of body and merry at heart. And I pray God heartily in his pleasure to continue the same. . . . My love, look what you will desire of me, whatsoever it be, and . . . I promise you by the help of our Lord to do it to [the best of] my power. . . . By your faithful Cousin and lover, Thomas Betson, I send you this ring for a token [of my love].[22]

The ideal of courtly love appears in numerous medieval manuscripts.

Eventually, Thomas and Katherine were married. She later repaid his genuine love and kind treatment by running his business and nursing him back to health when he became seriously ill.

Another loving marriage was that of a wealthy Frenchman, known to modern scholars as the Goodman of Paris, and his much younger wife. He wrote an entire book for her. It discusses her duties and the right way to run their house and estate, but it also reveals his deep love and respect for her.

"Know," he tells her, that all . . . you have done since we were wed until now and all that you shall do hereafter with good intent, was and is to my liking . . . and has well pleased me. . . . And know that I am pleased rather than displeased that you tend rose-trees, and care for violets, and

. . . dance, and sing. Nor would I have you cease to do so among our friends and equals, and it is but good and seemly so to pass the time of your youth. . . . I have confidence in your good intent.[23]

The Cult of Courtly Love

Thomas Betson, the Goodman of Paris, and men like them who clearly admired and genuinely loved and respected their wives seem to have felt that their wives had earned their affection by demonstrating their generosity, competence, loyalty, and love and respect for their husbands. Another medieval tradition painted a more general picture of women (specifically upper-class women) as ideal creatures to be put on pedestals without knowing their actual qualities.

Modern experts frequently refer to the literature, lore, and customs surrounding this curious aspect of the code of chivalry as the "cult of courtly love." Usually, courtly love had little or nothing to do with marriage. Rather, the object of a knight's or other courtier's love was a woman, either married or unmarried, on whom he desired to bestow compliments and expressions of love. As Bloch points out, like other aspects of the feudal system, courtly love was more about enacting formal rituals and ceremonies than about having a realistic relationship:

It always involved a strong emphasis of the man's adoration of the woman. It professed to be an all-engrossing passion, constantly frustrated, [and] easily jealous. . . . Its stereotyped development early acquired something of a ritual character. . . . [And] it was apt to express itself in terms borrowed from the vocabulary of vassal homage. And this was not merely a matter of words. The identification of the loved one and the lord correspond to an aspect of social morality entirely characteristic of feudal society.[24]

A fifteenth-century French manuscript shows a formal courting ceremony. The man swore to uphold the lady's honor, even if it meant losing his life.

Thus, some upper-class men and women actually went through elaborate ceremonies in which the beloved (the lady) formally accepted the adoration of the lover (the man). As in the ritual of vassal homage, the lover and beloved stood before witnesses and clasped hands. The man swore an oath to love the lady and defend her honor, even if it meant his death. She then gave him a ring and kissed him to acknowledge her acceptance. Numerous expressions of courtly love and the rituals surrounding it have survived. Among them are romantic songs composed by wandering troubadours. "I shall know no other love but hers," one begins.

> And if not her, no other love at all. She has surpassed all [other women]! So fair she is, so noble, I would be [her] captive. . . . God who has made all things in Earth that are, that made my love . . . grant me this grace, that I may some day come within a room, or in some garden gloom look her in the face. [25]

A man presents a love poem or song to the woman he is courting. Many love poems and songs from late medieval Europe have survived.

Working Women

As one might expect, the reality was that not all upper-class women could live up to the ideals perpetuated by the poets, troubadours, and knights. Another reality of medieval Europe was that upper-class women made up only a small percentage of the population. Most women were of lower economic means, the largest proportion being very poor, and they had no other choice but to work.

A great many women worked in and around their homes, performing a multitude of tasks on a daily and weekly basis. Among the more important and time consuming of these duties were spinning, weaving, and making clothes. Women also prepared and cooked food, helped harvest crops and feed farm animals, bought and sold necessary goods at markets, managed the servants and/or hired hands (if any), and performed first aid and healing, often using medicinal herbs. Usually the man of the house or the male farmer was the overall manager of the

Women spin wool into yarn. Almost all medieval women engaged in spinning and weaving.

home or farm. However, it was quite common for his wife (or mother or daughter if he was not married) to run the home or estate when he was gone on a military campaign. Thousands of women did so during the Crusades, a series of military/religious campaigns in which European armies traveled to Palestine to fight Muslims who had taken control of Jerusalem.

A group of medieval English women work in a local laundering business. On occasion, women owned as well as operated such businesses.

Some women, particularly poor and lower-middle-class women who dwelled in large towns and cities, also had paying jobs outside the home. Common female professions included spinning and weaving, making clothes, laundering, cleaning houses, and waiting tables in taverns. On occasion a woman might actually run a business (for instance, when her husband died and left her in charge), in which case she made the rules. In the vast majority of situations, however, women who worked outside the home had to adhere to set rules, which, of course, were formulated by men. Following are some of the rules of a women's crafts guild in thirteenth-century Paris:

> Any woman who wishes to be a silk spinner on large spindles in the city of Paris . . . may freely do so, provided she observes the following customs: No spinner on large spindles may have more than three apprentices unless they be her own or her husband's children. . . . If a working woman comes from outside Paris and wishes to practice the said craft in the city, she must swear before two [male] guardians . . . that she will practice it well and loyally. . . . If anyone give a woman of said craft silk to be spun and the woman pawn it and the owner complain, [she shall be fined].[26]

Nuns and Prioresses

In addition to the lower-class women who worked and the upper-class women who did not, some medieval European women decided to devote their lives to God. Unlike wives, mothers, female workers, and ladies of the court, nuns lived largely secluded, regimented lives behind the walls of convents. Much like other women in what was decidedly a man's world, however, nuns possessed little or no personal authority. In the eyes of the church, nuns were what might be called second-class servants of God. They were not equivalent to priests and were neither

Forced into the Convent

Not all medieval women who became nuns did so by choice. Sometimes a young woman's parents or guardians decided that it would be better for both her and them if she entered a convent. This is what happened to Madame Eglentyne, the prioress in Chaucer's Canterbury Tales. *The great scholar of medieval society Eileen Power tells what happened:*

Eglentyne became a nun because her father did not want the trouble and expense of finding her a husband, and because being a nun was about the only career for a well-born lady who did not marry. Moreover, by this time [the fourteenth century], monks and nuns had grown more lazy, and did little work with their hands and still less with their heads, particularly in nunneries, where the early tradition of learning had died out and where many nuns could hardly understand the Latin in which their services were written. The result was that the monastic life began to lose that essential variety which St. Benedict had designed for it, and as a result the regularity sometimes became irksome, and the series of services degenerated into a mere routine of peculiar monotony.

Eileen Power, *Medieval People.* New York: HarperCollins, 1992, p. 81.

trained nor allowed to administer sacraments such as Holy Communion and marriage.

Instead, it was understood that in taking their vows for the convent, nuns were submitting themselves completely, in body and soul, to the authority of the church that represented Christ on Earth. The average medieval nun endured endlessly repetitive rituals, much as male monks did. Also as in monasteries, the strict rules governing life in convents demanded silence most of the time. Except for a few very brief periods during the day, any necessary communication a nun made had to be in the form of sign language. One surviving document from a medieval convent contains 106 such signs.

The one nun in each convent who had some real authority, at least within that institution, was the prioress. The modern image of medieval prioresses has largely been shaped by the wonderful portrait Chaucer drew of one of them in his *Canterbury Tales.* He describes this character, Madame Eglentyne, as a reverent, clean, and neatly dressed woman with excellent manners and a generous spirit. "She was so charitable and piteous," Chaucer wrote, "that she would weep if she but saw a mouse caught in a trap, though it were dead or bled."[27] Probably because she had been on other religious pilgrimages, Madame Eglentyne was also fairly worldly and knowledgeable about secular life. It is revealing that she actually found the earthy and irreverent Wife of Bath charming. Perhaps they and most other women of their time and place recognized a sort of underlying, unspoken bond or kinship. The fact was that regardless of background, social rank, or profession, they were all struggling to find whatever relevance and fulfillment they could in a world ruled by men.

Chapter Five

MERCHANTS AND TRADERS: THE ART OF MAKING MONEY

Merchants and traders were a rare commodity in the early medieval era, far fewer in number than farmers, serfs, members of landed families, and ordinary townspeople. This was mainly because at first, most towns and large estates were fairly small and isolated from one another. In the wake of the destruction of the Roman Empire by tribal peoples from central and northern Europe, many cities were sacked, communities were fragmented, and commerce in general diminished considerably in the disrupted subsistence economy.

Crafts and trades continued at a local level, however, as social conditions stabilized and gave rise to shops owned and run by merchants and usually concentrated in towns. Thereafter, such local production for local consumption represented the first of the two principal aspects of medieval commerce. The second was trade, at first between neighboring towns and districts, and eventually among foreign cities and kingdoms. The economic need for and development of long-range commerce created a growing class of traders (traveling merchants). The great early twentieth-century Belgian scholar Henri Pirenne ably described the origins of these men who were destined to play such an important role in medieval society:

> [They] were originally recruited from among landless men, who lived, so to speak, on the margin of a society where land alone was the basis of existence. . . . The younger sons of a man over-burdened with children were often forced to [strike out on their own, and] they swelled the crowd of vagabonds who roamed

through the country . . . hiring themselves out [as farm helpers, soldiers, sailors, and dock workers]. The savings of a little peddler, a sailor . . . or a docker furnished him with quite enough capital [money], if only he knew how to use it. . . . With luck, the best among [such men] could not fail to seize the many opportunities . . . which commercial life offered to . . . [those] who threw themselves into it with energy and intelligence.[28]

Such enterprising individuals, who saw the potential of buying and selling raw materials and craft goods, were further

A painting dating from late medieval France shows merchants inspecting barrels of wine. Merchants were members of a small middle class.

High Praise for Merchants

Medieval merchants and traders naturally tried to promote themselves and their profession to potential customers as well as to society in general. This obviously biased statement of praise for merchants was composed by an Italian trader in 1458:

The dignity and office of merchants is great and exalted in many respects. First . . . the advancement of public welfare is a very honorable purpose. . . . The advancement, the comfort, and the health of [countries] to a large extent proceed from [the efforts of] merchants. . . . And with respect to mercantile business and activity . . . [it] also brings about an abundance of money, jewels, gold, silver, and all kinds of metals. . . . Cities and countries are driven to cultivate the land, to enlarge the herds, and to exploit the incomes and rents. And [merchants] through their activity enable the poor to live. . . . Neither kings nor princes, nor any other rank of men enjoy as much reputation or credit as a good merchant.

Quoted in R.S. Lopez and I.W. Raymond, *Medieval Trade in the Mediterranean World.* New York: Columbia University Press, 1955, pp. 416–18.

Fruit and grain merchants ply their trade in fifteenth-century Italy. Some successful merchants exported goods across the entire Mediterranean area.

inspired by exposure to new foods, goods, and knowledge brought back from the Crusades, and by the rise of stable European currencies over the old barter system. Their success spearheaded the growth of a small but economically viable middle class, beginning in the 1100s. Middle-class merchants were better off than the peasants but usually not as well-off as the nobles. A few merchants and traders grew rich, however, and rivaled the traditional aristocrats in wealth and influence. Some of these successful businessmen became wealthy bankers, who lent money not only to traders, but to people of all walks of life. Thus, by the thirteenth century, commerce and the merchant class were well established and thriving in Europe.

From Temporary Stalls to Permanent Shops

The first successful medieval businessmen were merchants who bought crops, livestock, wool, clothes, craft items, or other materials produced in the nearby countryside and sold them in the towns. They usually set up movable stalls (often consisting of large wagons or tents) in markets held once or twice a week in town squares or in other open spaces in the towns. Noted scholar Marjorie Rowling gives a colorful description of such a market:

> Before the stalls displaying fresh fish . . . a [man] from a neighboring estate might be seen bargaining for his lord. At another [stall would be] an overseer buying butcher's meat,

honey, salt, oil, butter, cheese, fruit, and wine for his daughter's wedding feast. Meanwhile, the girl herself, with her mother, might be haggling over the cost of . . . bridal garments. . . . At another stall, peasants might be inspecting knives for pruning vines . . . or spades for digging. Nearby, a display of . . . cowhide, from which shoes could be made, would attract its own purchasers. [29]

Over time, many merchants made enough money to replace their movable stalls with permanent versions. In other words, they built or rented space for shops that were open for business on a daily rather than weekly basis. It became customary in most towns for most or all of the shops selling a certain product to occupy one street or sector; thus, there was often a butchers' district, a drapers' (fabric-sellers') district, or a goldsmiths' district.

Those local merchants who were most successful bought or built large, comfortable homes. In most cases, their new upper-middle-class lifestyle contrasted sharply with the poverty they knew growing up. A twelfth-century Italian document describes two poor boys who became wealthy merchants in northern Italy:

> Sceva and Ollo were . . . boys of low birth [who] acquired at the same time a small capital [pool of money], and in our days became first hawkers of small commodities, then by continued success, of large ones. From pack-

men, they arose to be carriers, from that to masters of many wagons, and always remained trusty partners.[30]

Another successful merchant, Jean Boine Broke, ran a thriving fabric business in Flanders in the late 1200s. He owned a very large house, which he used as a factory, office, and warehouse as well as his residence. He employed many workers, who sorted raw wool, combed and oiled it, and dyed it. Some of his customers placed special orders for bolts of fabric of certain qualities and colors; others came to his warehouse and bought products right off the shelves.

The Rise of Wealthy Mercantile Families

Men like Sceva, Ollo, and Broke usually passed on their businesses to their sons (and in rare cases to their daughters), who, conditions permitting, continued to expand them. Some European families grew quite wealthy and influential this way. The most famous examples were the leading mercantile families of Venice (in northeastern Italy), the greatest trading city of the Middle Ages. There, and in some other large cities, a few of these fortunate families formed a sort of new nobility that rivaled that of the traditional aristocrats.

One reason these rich family businesses were so successful for so long was that they learned to control most of the production processes of the goods they traded. First they obtained the raw materials

A Trader Disputes a Price

Sometimes medieval traders were forced to dispute the prices of room and board when they were away on business trips. These are excerpts from a letter written home by an English trader named William Cely in the late 1400s, in which he complains about a host who tried to charge too much:

There is a variance between our host Thomas Graunger ... for [he] promised us ... that we should pay no more for our board [food] but 3 shillings, 4 pence [pennies] a week at the high table ... and now he says he will have no less than 4 shillings a week at the high table. [In protest, my fellow merchants] will depart into other lodgings, some to one place and some to another.

Quoted in H.E. Malden, ed., *The Cely Papers, Selected from the Correspondence and Memoranda of the Cely Family, Merchants of the Staple.* Camden, UK: Royal Historical Society, 1900, p. 135.

(such as wool or precious metals); then they hired and trained the workers who turned these materials into salable products; and finally, they sold the finished products for large profits.

Considering the enormous fortunes these wealthy mercantile families accumulated, it is not surprising that they eventually learned to make money from money itself. Such families, particularly

French coal merchants transport bags of coal in an illustration in a publication distributed by a local merchant guild. Such guilds operated in every city.

in the Italian cities of Venice, Florence, Naples, Genoa, and Rome, operated financial firms that lent money to various merchants and nobles and charged hefty interest on the loans. Among the leaders in the rise of banking was the powerful Medici family, based in Florence. The Medicis operated banking branches in other Italian cities, as well as London and Paris.

Merchant Guilds

The wealthy mercantile families were not the only organizations that controlled and influenced medieval production and commerce, however. These families recognized the powers exercised by so-called merchant guilds, regulatory and protective associations that emerged across the continent. Eventually there was a guild for practically every craft and mercantile activity—guilds for grocers, spinners and weavers, drapers, metalworkers, candle makers, and so forth.

These organizations helped their members in a number of ways. First, they helped to safeguard their financial interests, so that aristocrats and wealthy manufacturers did not take advantage of them. When possible, they banded together to set fair prices on raw materials, for example. Guilds also functioned as social and charitable organizations in a society in which there were many destitute homeless, jobless, or elderly persons. If a metalworker fell ill and could not work, for instance, his guild might help him support his family during the crisis. Merchant guilds also paid for the funerals of those members whose families could not afford them. And such funerals were always well attended. One of the rules listed in the official ordinance of a guild in Southampton, England, stated:

> When a guildsman dies, all those who are of the guild shall attend the service of the dead, and guildsmen shall bear the body and bring it to the place of burial. And whoever [in the guild] will not do this, shall pay

Many medieval merchant guilds produced illustrations depicting their members at work. This one was made by the Venetian Weavers' Guild.

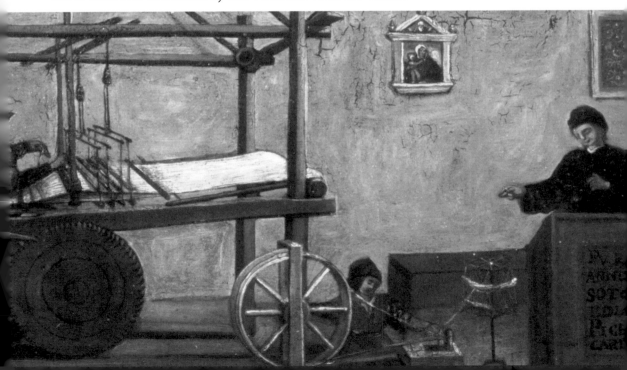

. . . two pence, to be given to the poor. . . . And so long as the service of the dead shall last . . . there ought to burn four candles of the guild, each candle of two pounds weight or more. [31]

Guild members also frequently traveled together in groups in order to help keep them safe from thieves and pirates.

Traveling Traders

The merchants who were most at the mercy of attacks by such criminals were the long-range traders who traveled far and wide buying and selling a wide range of goods. By the year 1000, traders had established themselves in many parts of Europe. And in the following two centuries the more enterprising of their number boldly opened up new markets in remote regions that had long been isolated from Europe's growing economic mainstream.

One of these pioneering traders about whom evidence has survived was an Italian, Corrado of Ora. In 1236 he reached the remote town of Tessero, in northern Italy. He met with some of the leading citizens and struck a deal with a landowner named Otto Grasso. For a set price, Ora promised to keep Grasso (and per-

This illustration was part of a sign made by the Venetian Boat Builders' Guild in 1517. It shows several ships under construction.

haps his neighbors) supplied with high-quality beans, rye, millet, and herbs grown in other parts of Italy on a yearly basis for as long as needed.

Among the other medieval traders, one of the best known was an English wool merchant named Thomas Betson—the same man who expressed his love for his fiancée in an often-quoted letter. (In fact, almost all we know about Betson comes from a group of his letters that fortunately survived.) Betson's eventual wife was the daughter of another well-to-do wool trader, William Stoner. In his business, Betson bought wool from English sheep ranchers and had the wool cleaned. Then, with the aid of his apprentices, he packed the merchandise and delivered it in person to buyers in northern France and more distant locales.

During such business trips, Betson and his fellow traders were always on the lookout for pirates and other criminals intent on stealing their valuable goods. Pirates plied their disreputable trade along most of Europe's coasts. But they were especially numerous in waters frequented by merchant vessels, such as the English Channel. A number of traders' letters have survived informing loved ones, backers, or customers that the goods made it through safely. One, penned by Englishman Thomas Henham, states: "I departed from Sandwich the 11th day of April and so came into Calais [in northern France] upon Shrove Thursday last with the wool ships, and so blessed be Jesus [that] I have received your wools in safety!"[32]

Traders like Ora, Betson, and Henham naturally had to find places to stay when they were away on business in foreign lands. Betson reveals in his letters that he often found lodgings in the homes of local people who made businesses of their own by renting out rooms to traveling merchants. Along with religious pilgrims and other travelers, merchants also sometimes found accommodations in hospices run by monks. These were small sections of monasteries set aside to lodge people in need of a place to spend the night. A merchant might also stay in the manor houses or castles of some of his well-to-do customers, where he would dine with them and tell them about recent events in his native land. In addition, there were inns located at intervals along Europe's major roads. And finally, local merchant guilds often ran inexpensive hostels that welcomed less well-off merchants, as well as poor religious pilgrims. One such establishment is mentioned in a surviving English public record dating from 1340: "The Guild Merchant of Coventry provided a hostel with thirteen beds. . . . A governor [manager] presided over it, and there was a woman to keep it clean. The upkeep was £10 a year."[33]

The International Fairs

Although the busiest traders, including Betson, sometimes had individual customers they serviced on a regular basis, a large portion of their business was transacted at international fairs. These were well-known gatherings of traders that took

Among the many international fairs held in medieval Europe was the Lendit Fair, near St. Denis in north-central France.

place annually in various northern European locales. Some of the largest fairs were held in Flanders, Switzerland, Germany, and England. A typical fair lasted from one to six weeks, during which time the attending traders had to find whatever lodgings they could in the area. As happens today when a large convention is held in a city, finding a vacant room was difficult, so many of the traders had to rough it in tents. Such events could be colorful and exciting, except when the weather turned foul. An Englishman who attended the Westminster Fair, held one year in southern England during the often chilly and raw rainy season, recalled:

All the merchants, in exposing their goods for sale there, had no shelter except canvas tents; owing to the changeable gusts of wind assailing them . . . they were cold and wet, and also suffered from hunger and thirst; their feet were soiled by mud, and their goods rotted by the showers of rain. [34]

The traders naturally tried to dress according to the weather, as well as to look their best for potential buyers. Excerpts from Betson's letters reveal that his outfits varied according to the season in which a fair was held. In the winter, for what was called the "cold mart," he decked himself out in furs; whereas at the "Pask mart" in the spring, he wore lighter clothes and stuck a flower in his cap.

Merchants of all types gathered at the international fairs. These trade shows offered opportunities to sell goods and gain new customers.

Betson's letters also talk about some of the deals he struck with customers and the manner in which he was paid. In the centuries before he was born, merchants and traders received either money, in the form of gold or silver coins, or barter (goods exchanged for goods). But by Betson's day, a supplementary form of payment had emerged at the international fairs (as well as in the larger towns), namely, buying on credit. In this new system, a customer could take possession of the goods and promise to pay the seller later. Similarly, rich bankers extended credit to traders like Betson when they were short of cash. In such a deal, the merchant signed a promissory note, in which he promised to pay the asking price of the goods, plus interest, in a set number of months.

Sometimes the use of credit could cause unwanted delays and anxiety. In Betson's case, for instance, he often purchased wool from English ranchers on credit and promised to pay them within six months. But on the other end of the deal, sometimes his customers took their time paying him. If he could not repay his creditors when the six months were up, he would have to pay additional interest, or he might lose these ranchers to another trader. In the end, profit was the bottom line. In Europe's emerging capitalist society, everyone—sellers, buyers, and traders alike—had to have money to live. Unbeknownst to Betson and his contemporaries, the art of making and accumulating money was laying the foundations of the market economy and modern society that would inevitably sweep away the feudal system and medieval culture with it.

Chapter Six

SCHOLARS, ARTISTS, AND EXPLORERS: REMAKING THE WORLD

As was the case with successful merchants and traders, few scholars, philosophers, artists, inventors, explorers, and other educated, inquisitive individuals existed in Europe in the early centuries of the medieval era. The collapse of the Roman Empire in the fifth and sixth centuries had left the continent not only politically fragmented, but largely poverty-stricken and culturally backward. Indeed, the first few centuries following Rome's demise are often called the "Dark Ages."

This term has been overused and overdramatized; modern experts debate just how "dark" the era was for civilization in general. Yet there is widespread agreement that these centuries did witness a low ebb of learning and intellectual and creative endeavors in Europe. Very few people could read and write. And for the most part, the advanced philosophical and scientific traditions of the Greeks (and to a lesser degree the Romans) had been lost.

In time, however, this rather bleak situation changed. Learning was revived in Europe and the number of educated individuals and intellectuals in society increased (though they long remained a small minority of the population). This revival was led by a tiny but highly influential group of thinkers, writers, and artists, some affiliated with the churches and others secular, who began to look at the world and the role of humans within it in new ways. Their ideas further stimulated the spread and expansion of schools, education, and learning, as well as the arts, new building designs and techniques, philosophical and scientific ideas, and ultimately exploration of the wide world lying beyond European borders.

Some of the new ideas that began to spread across Europe in the early years of the second millennium were borrowed from Arabic scholars who lived and worked in prosperous, more culturally advanced cities in the Near East (now called the Middle East). They had been largely unaffected by Rome's fall, and they had maintained the writings of Aristotle and other leading ancient Greek thinkers, mostly in Arabic translations. A few better-educated European knights and priests who traveled to Palestine managed to acquire some of these ancient Greek works; others initiated searches for old manuscripts in European cities. The rediscovery by Europeans of their own ancient intellectual heritage in the 1100s and 1200s was an important milestone in Europe's development. Stimulated by the ideas of the past, a number of thinkers began building on them and developing fresh approaches to learning and artistic expression.

These energetic intellectual activities became a major factor in the emergence of what modern scholars call the High Middle Ages and the Renaissance. Lasting from about 1300 to 1600, the European Renaissance began in Italy and rapidly spread to other countries. During this last period of medieval times, edu-

A thirteenth-century Arabic manuscript depicts the Greek thinker Aristotle lecturing his students. The Arabs preserved ancient Greek learning.

cated individuals began to reject traditional, rigid ideas about the world and humanity's place in it and to embrace more modern ways of thinking. This included new ways of looking at religion and financial dealings. In addition, writers and artists produced a huge outburst of creativity. Great literary works, magnificent paintings, and huge buildings with imposing architecture were produced, especially in Italy. In this way, it was the thinkers and artists, not the monarchs and military generals, who steadily remade the medieval world and in so doing gave rise to the modern era.

Teachers, Scholars, and Education

Medieval Europe's flowering of great thinkers, builders, and artists was built not only on the rediscovery of old ideas, but also on the tireless efforts of generations of their medieval predecessors. The forerunners of the giants of the Renaissance were more modest individuals who learned to read and write, and pursued knowledge, at a time when getting a decent education was difficult and rare. In the early centuries of the medieval era, a very small minority of people were educated. Most of them were either monks and priests or the children of aristocrats who attended the schools run by the monks. Only a tiny handful of lower-class children managed to get into these schools and obtain educations. So most people remained illiterate and the few scholars who existed were monks who

A painting dating from 1395 shows a Jewish teacher and one of his pupils. Like Christian monks, Jewish scholars copied books and passed on knowledge.

collected, read, and copied texts within the walls of their monasteries.

The monastery schools remained the mainstay of education until about 1100 or so. In the years that followed, stimulated by the growing rediscovery of ancient knowledge, more and more schools run by the secular clergy opened.

Origins of the Liberal Arts Curriculum

The medieval educational tradition of teaching the so-called Seven Liberal Arts was inspired by the rediscovered writings of a few late Greco-Roman scholars. Among them was a Roman civil servant named Cassiodorus. In 540, in the wake of the disintegration of the Roman Empire, he retired from public life and established a monastery in southern Italy. Upset over the destruction of old books in the barbarian invasions of the preceding century, he trained a group of monks in the task of copying the old manuscripts he had rescued. Though he was a devout Christian, Cassiodorus was an open-minded scholar who believed that secular knowledge was valuable, too. He summarized a great deal of that knowledge, including many aspects of Greco-Roman science, in his

work titled *On Training in Sacred and Profane Literature.* Along with an encyclopedia by the fifth-century Roman scholar Martianus Capella, this book established the educational canon of liberal arts that became standard in the Middle Ages and European Renaissance.

This version of Aristotle's Physics *appeared in the 1300s, during Europe's rediscovery of ancient Greco-Roman knowledge.*

And the number of students enrolled in one kind of school or another significantly increased. As time went on, these schools taught more than simply reading and writing. Inspired by the writings of a few late Greco-Roman scholars, medieval teachers increasingly stressed the Seven Liberal Arts. Among others, these included geometry, astronomy (which still promoted the idea that the sun revolved around Earth), rhetoric (the art of persuasive speaking), and music.

A number of the church schools teaching the liberal arts rapidly expanded. And by 1300 some of them had grown into full-fledged universities. Among the leading universities were those in the Italian cities of Salerno and Bologna, the French cities of Paris and Toulouse, and the English town of Oxford. Some of the professors, called "masters," who taught at these institutions were churchmen; but a growing number were highly educated laymen. These masters formed their own professional guilds, similar to those of merchants and craftsmen. The university masters became widely respected not only for their knowledge, but also as intellectual and moral role models for young men seeking higher education. Some idea of the strict qualifications required to teach in the major universities comes from a list of regulations issued in 1215 for the University of Paris:

> No one shall lecture in the [liberal] arts at Paris before he is twenty-one years of age, and he shall have heard lectures for at least six years before he begins to lecture. . . . He shall not be stained by any infamy [disreputable acts], and when he is ready to lecture, he shall be examined according to the form . . . [approved by] the chancellor [director of the school] and [a panel of distinguished] scholars. [35]

The frequent use of the word *lecture* in this and other similar documents indicates that lecturing (with the students taking

A monk named Amalric of Bena lectures at the University of Paris during the Renaissance. Instructors at such universities were widely respected.

The Glories of Medieval Church Decoration

One of Europe's chief intellectual and artistic centers in the High Middle Ages was Germany. There, a skilled metalworker and builder named Roger Helmershausen, who used the pseudonym Theophilus, penned a treatise titled On Divers Arts. *Among other things, he described the beautiful and inspirational work then occurring in church building and decoration:*

You [craftsmen and artists] have embellished the ceilings and walls with varied work in different colors, and have, in some measure shown to beholders the paradise of God.... You have given them cause to praise the Creator.... For the human eye is not able to consider on what work first to fix its gaze.... If it beholds the ceilings, they glow like brocades.... If it regards the profusion of light from the windows, it marvels at the ... beauty of the [stained] glass and the infinitely rich and varied workmanship.

Theophilus, *On Divers Arts,* trans. C.R. Dodwell. London: Thomas Nelson, 1961, p. 49.

It is my purpose to teach you faithfully and in a kindly manner ... [that] has customarily been observed by the ancient and modern [masters] and particularly by my [own] master. First, I shall give you the summaries of each [law book] title before I come to the text. Second, I shall put forth well and distinctly ... the purpose of each law. Third, I shall read the text in order to correct it. Fourth, I shall briefly restate the meaning. [36]

Europe's Master Builders

In addition to laymen teachers, by the thirteenth century laymen began to supplement the ranks of monks who had long dominated the fields of building and art. For some time to come, however, the builders' styles and the artists' subjects were supplied by the Christian church and its imagery and traditions. This was because nearly everyone in medieval Europe was religiously devout and religious themes pervaded all levels of society. Indeed, the vast majority of builders, painters, sculptors, and other artists not only regularly employed these themes, but also followed traditional guidelines supplied by the church. Most adhered, without question, to a dictate set down by a congress of bishops in the eighth century. "The composition of religious imagery," it stated, "is not left to the initiative of the artists, but is formed upon principles laid down by the Catholic Church and by religious tradition." [37]

notes) was the standard teaching method in these schools. The manner in which the masters lectured was described by Odofredus, a master who taught a course on law at the University of Bologna in the 1250s:

The most lavish way for builders and artists to show their love and respect for God was to erect churches, thousands of which appeared in Europe during the Middle Ages. The earliest known medieval builder for whom sufficient evidence survives was a French Benedictine monk named Airardus. He likely created the cathedral at Saint Denis, in France, which later became a model for many other European churches. Airardus and other men with similar talents were not architects in the modern sense; that is, they did not draw up precise blueprints for a structure and hand them over to professional construction crews to follow. Rather, the early medieval version of an architect was a jack-of-all-trades who conceived of a general design and made it a reality by overseeing all aspects of the construction process, including the artistic decorations. The overseer of a wooden building was called a master-carpenter; for a stone structure, one hired a master mason.

As time went on, European master builders, especially those in France,

A fourteenth-century rendering shows French king Louis VI watching masons work on a new church.

invented a new style of architecture. The older churches, in the Romanesque style, had small windows that let in limited amounts of light. The keys to the newer style—Gothic—were structural elements (including the flying buttress and ribbed vault) that allowed builders to erect stronger, higher walls; these allowed the placement of large stained-glass windows that flooded the vast interiors with light, greatly inspiring churchgoers, nobles and peasants alike. Thus were born the splendid spires of Notre Dame, Chartres, Rheims, and other Gothic marvels.

Humanism and the Renaissance

While most builders, artists, and other creative individuals were perpetuating religious ideals in their work, a few educated people began to realize that human virtues do not derive from formal religion alone. These more liberal thinkers

Educated thinkers like those in this fifteenth-century rendering increasingly concluded that human beings are inherently worthy creatures.

were inspired not only by the artistic and literary values of the ancient thinkers, but also by their philosophical ideas. On the one hand, the new thinkers said, Greek and Roman architecture, painting, and music should be studied and imitated; on the other, Europeans needed to recognize an important truth that Aristotle and other ancient thinkers had recognized: the inherent dignity of human beings and their ability to be virtuous and creative by their own initiative. Those European intellectuals and artists who embraced this philosophy believed that it was not necessary to invoke mystical or divine forces to find the truths of life and the universe. Instead, they said, these truths could be discovered by the human mind using reason, logic, and diligent study.

The members of this movement, which emerged in the final years of the Middle Ages, called themselves humanists, from the Latin term *humanitas,* meaning "humanity." Among the leading humanist thinkers and writers were Germany's Desiderius Erasmus, Italy's Francesco Petrarch, France's François Rabelais, and England's Thomas More. Most of these men and the other humanists remained devoutly religious (although a few of the later humanists questioned the worth and authority of religion). But they argued that formal religion, with its strict rules and devotion to tradition, often limited the use of a gift God had bestowed on humans—the potential to learn and create new things. It actually glorified God, some humanists argued, for humans to use the mental tools he had given them

Francesco Petrarch (1304–1374) was among Europe's leading medieval humanists.

in the pursuit of knowledge and ways to enrich society.

The Renaissance was therefore a period in which a small but supremely talented and influential group of individuals introduced new ideas and produced an immense outburst of cultural expression and achievement. In addition to philosophers such as Erasmus and Petrarch, there were so-called "civic humanists." They tried to improve the quality of government in or to beautify their cities. In Florence, for example, a

Leonardo Applies for a Job

It surprises many people today to learn that many of the artistic and scientific geniuses of the medieval world spent much of their time traveling around looking for work. This was the case with one of the greatest of them all—Leonardo da Vinci. Following is an excerpt from the résumé he submitted when he applied for a job with the ruler of the Italian city of Milan in 1493.

I shall endeavor . . . to explain myself to your Excellency. . . . I have [invented] many machines most efficient for [military] offense and defense, and vessels which will resist the attack of the largest guns. . . . In case of [your] need, I will make big guns, mortars, and . . . catapults. . . . In time of peace I . . . can [design] buildings, public and private. . . . I can carry out sculpture in marble, bronze, and clay, and I also can do in painting whatever may [need to] be done. . . . If any of the above-mentioned things seem to

anyone to be impossible . . . I am most ready to [demonstrate them] in whatever place may please your Excellency.

Leonardo da Vinci, *The Literary Works of Leonardo da Vinci*, Jean Paul Richter and Irma A. Richter, eds. New York: Oxford University Press, 1939, pp. 325–27.

A section of one of Leonardo's masterpieces—The Virgin of the Rocks *(ca. 1508).*

scholar named Leon Battista Alberti (1404–1472) designed and erected magnificent buildings. Alberti personified the image of the "Renaissance man," a highly versatile person possessing many intellectual, artistic, and other talents. He was a gifted musician, poet, and athlete, as well as a builder. His younger Italian contemporary, Leonardo da Vinci (1452–1519), achieved even greater fame for his skills as a painter, sculptor, engineer, and inventor.

No less brilliant and accomplished was still another Italian, Michelangelo Buonarotti (1475–1564), universally recognized as the greatest artist of the Renaissance. He is most famous for the series of paintings he executed on the ceiling of the Sistine Chapel, in the Vatican in Rome. These splendid images show the creation of the world as envisioned in the biblical Book of Genesis, highlighted by a dramatic scene of God giving Adam, the first human being, the gift of life.

Scientists and Explorers

While great artists such as Michelangelo were depicting how the world supposedly came to be, other learned Europeans were describing its shape and arguing over its place in the universe. Aristotle and other ancient Greek scholars knew Earth was round, and medieval scholars inherited this knowledge. (The idea that medieval people thought Earth was flat is a myth.) However, throughout the Middle Ages nearly everyone mistakenly believed that the planet occupied the center of creation. In the 1300s, the note mathematician Nicole Oresme declared: "The Earth is round like a ball . . . and [lies] at the center of the universe because it is the heaviest of the four elements."[38]

In fact, the realization that Earth actually revolves around the sun, proposed by Polish astronomer Nicolas Copernicus in 1543, marked the beginning of the emergence of the modern science of astronomy. And that emergence was itself one of the principal boundary markers between the medieval and modern worlds. One factor that made medieval scholars medieval, after all, was their almost blind acceptance of the concept of a geocentric (Earth-centered) universe. Both Aristotle and the Bible supported this idea; and Aristotle and the Bible were far and away the two most widely accepted and venerated authorities in the medieval era. When Copernicus, the Italian scholar Galileo, and other brilliant thinkers showed that these authorities had been wrong about Earth's place in the universe, the medieval world view began to collapse.

Another development that signaled the end of the medieval world was the discovery of previously unknown continents lying beyond Europe's western and eastern horizons. Even as Copernicus and Galileo introduced the sun-centered universe, European explorers landed in North and South America and other lands distant from Europe. These developments would not have been possible without the cumulative efforts of medieval scientists and technicians, which made long voyages in the open, uncharted seas possible. Among them were astronomers, mathematicians, inventors, mapmakers, and naval engineers, especially those brought together by a Portuguese nobleman known as Prince Henry the Navigator. These clever individuals, noted historian William H. McNeill points out, constructed simple astronomical instruments and [mathematical] tables by which ship captains could measure the latitude of newly discovered places . . . [allowing] the Portuguese to make usable charts of the Atlantic coasts. . . . At the same time, Portuguese naval experts attacked the problem of improving ship construction. [They] rapidly improved seaworthiness, maneuverability, and speed of Portuguese and . . . other European ships. . . . Other innovations allowed a crew to trim the sails to suit varying conditions of wind and sea, thus greatly facilitating steering and protecting the vessel from disaster in sudden gales. [39]

Thanks to these advances, the Portuguese established valuable colonies and trading posts on Africa's western coast in the early-to-mid-1400s. Then Portuguese navigator Bartholomew Dias sailed around the Cape of Good Hope, on Africa's southern tip, in 1488. And in 1492 Christopher Columbus, an Italian sailing for Spain, made it to the West Indies. In the years that followed, European explorers reached Central America, Florida, India, China, and Japan.

These explorations opened up vast new territories for settlement and economic exploitation. Several of Europe's once small and largely insular feudal kingdoms were now emerging as prosperous, enterprising nations—England, France, Spain, and others—on a global stage. The modern era had begun. And the world of lords and their landed vassals, of serfs and wandering troubadours, and of knights pursuing ladies in the cult of courtly love was rapidly fading into the mists of time. It had been largely inquisitive minds of medieval educators, philosophers, artists, engineers, scientists, and explorers that had made this transition possible. They had eagerly sought to know the truth about their place in the grander scheme of things. What they did not realize was that finding that truth would bring about the end of their society and replace it with a world they could scarcely dream of.

Notes

Introduction: Medieval People: The Harsh Realities of Their World

1. James F. Dunnigan and Albert A. Nofi, in "Just War," *Medieval Life & the Hundred Years War*, p. 2. www.hyw.com/books/history/war _just.htm.

Chapter One: Kings, Vassals, and Serfs: The Feudal Order

2. Marjorie Rowling, *Everyday Life in Medieval Times*. New York: Berkley, 1987, pp. 32–33.
3. Quoted in Brian Tierney, ed., *The Middle Ages*, vol. 1, *Sources of Medieval History*. New York: McGraw-Hill, 1998, p. 128.
4. Quoted in Tierney, *The Middle Ages*, p. 125.
5. Quoted in Carl Stephenson and Frederick G. Marcham, eds., *Sources of English Constitutional History: A Selection of Documents from A.D. 600 to the Interregnum*. New York: Haper & Row, 1972, p. 58.
6. Quoted in Eugen Weber, ed., *The Western Tradition: From the Ancient World to Louis XIV*. Lexington, MA: D.C. Heath, 1995, p. 214.

7. Quoted in Joseph Gies and Frances Gies, *Life in a Medieval Castle*. New York: Harper & Row, 1979, pp. 57–58.
8. Quoted in Tierney, *The Middle Ages*, pp. 283–84.
9. Quoted in J.H. Robinson, trans., *Translations and Reprints from the Original Sources of European History*, vol. 3. Philadelphia: University of Pennsylvania Press, 1912, pp. 4–5.

Chapter Two: Soldiers: Risking and Losing Life and Limb

10. Marc Bloch, *Feudal Society*, trans. L.A. Manyon. London: Routledge, 1989, pp. 304–305.
11. Quoted in Bloch, *Feudal Society*, p. 293.
12. Quoted in Rowling, *Everyday Life in Medieval Times*, p. 40.
13. Quoted in Weber, *Western Tradition*, p. 215.

Chapter Three: People of Faith: Hearts and Minds Devoted to God

14. Bloch, *Feudal Society*, p. 80.

15. Walther Kirchner, *Middle Ages, 375–1492*. New York: Barnes & Noble, 1968, pp. 91–92.

16. Paul Johnson, *A History of Christianity*. New York: Atheneum, 1976, pp. 146–47.

17. Quoted in Tierney, *Middle Ages*, p. 114.

18. Quoted in Tierney, *Middle Ages*, pp. 144–45.

Chapter Four: Women: Doing Their Duties in a Man's World

19. Pauline Stafford, "Powerful Women in the Early Middle Ages," in *The Medieval World*, ed. Peter Linehan and Janet L. Nelson, London: Routledge, 2001, p. 399.

20. Quoted in Rowling, *Everyday Life in Medieval Times*, p. 72.

21. Quoted in Rowling, *Everyday Life in Medieval Times*, pp. 72–73.

22. Quoted in Eileen Power, *Medieval People*. New York: HarperPerennial, 1992, pp. 127–29.

23. Quoted in Eileen Power, trans., *The Goodman of Paris*. Woodbridge, UK: Boydell, 2006, p. 33.

24. Bloch, *Feudal Society*, p. 309.

25. Jaufre Rudel, "To His Love Afar," in *The Wandering Scholars*, trans. Helen Waddell. Mineola, NY: Dover, 2000, p. 206.

26. Quoted in Tierney, *Middle Ages*, p. 190.

27. Geoffrey Chaucer, *The Canterbury Tales*, trans. J.U. Nicolson, in *Great Books of the Western World*, vol. 19, *Dante and Chaucer*. Chicago: Encyclopaedia Britannica, 1952, p. 161.

Chapter Five: Merchants and Traders: The Art of Making Money

28. Henri Pirenne, *Economic and Social History of Medieval Europe*, trans. L.E. Clegg. New York: Harcourt, Brace, 1956, pp. 46–48.

29. Rowling, *Everyday Life in Medieval Times*, p. 55.

30. Quoted in Rowling, *Everyday Life in Medieval Times*, p. 60.

31. Quoted in Weber, *Western Tradition*, p. 280.

32. Quoted in Power, *Medieval People*, p. 143.

33. Quoted in *Chaucer's World*. Clair C. Olson and Martin M. Chow, eds., New York: Columbia University Press, 1948, p. 269.

34. Quoted in Roy C. Cave and Herbert H. Coulson, *A Source Book for Medieval Economic History*. Milwaukee: Bruce, 1936, p. 125.

Chapter Six: Scholars, Artists, and Explorers: Remaking the World

35. Quoted in Lynn Thorndike, *University Records and Life in the Mid-*

dle Ages. New York: Columbia University Press, 1944, p. 28.

36. Quoted in Tierney, *Middle Ages,* pp. 294–95.

37. Quoted in Rowling, *Everyday Life in Medieval Times,* p. 156.

38. Quoted in Rowling, *Everyday Life in Medieval Times,* p. 203.

39. W.H. McNeill, *The Rise of the West.* New York: New American Library, 1963, pp. 624–25.

Glossary

cavalry (or **cavalrymen**): Mounted soldiers.

coif: A cap or head protector made of metal or mail, worn by knights and some other medieval soldiers.

fealty: Loyalty.

friar: In the Middle Ages, a member of a monastic order who dedicated himself to poverty and going out into the community and preaching to and helping those in need.

Gothic: A style of art and architecture that developed in Europe during the medieval period; it was characterized by its use of flying buttresses, ribbed vaults, towering spires, and elaborate stained-glass windows.

great hall (or **hall**): The principal living quarters of a medieval castle or house.

guild: In medieval times, a union-like trade organization that looked after the interests of its members in both their jobs and private lives.

homage: The ceremony in which a vassal swore loyalty to his lord.

humanism: An intellectual and artistic movement that developed during the European Renaissance; the humanists believed that people could create great art and literature and uncover the truths of the universe through the inherent powers of the human mind and spirit.

infantry (or **infantrymen**): Foot soldiers.

lance: A group of knights and their servants and other followers, usually from a single manor, who assembled for military service.

manor: An estate held by a lord and farmed by his tenants and serfs.

manorial system: The arrangement whereby a lord allowed serfs and other workers to farm portions of his land, in return for which they gave him a share of their harvests and performed various duties and services.

master mason: In medieval times, a combination of architect, building contractor, and general overseer for a structure made of stone; a wooden structure was overseen by a master carpenter.

masters: Professors at medieval universities and other schools of higher learning.

mercantile: Having to do with commerce, merchants, and making money.

monk: In the Middle Ages, a member of a monastic order who spent much of his time secluded in a monastery (although some monks traveled to do missionary work).

papal: Having to do with the popes who have long overseen the Roman Catholic Church.

pilgrimage: A journey; in medieval times, the term most often referred to a trip made to a religious shrine of some kind.

prioress: The head nun and director of a priory, or convent.

priory: A convent.

retinue: A group of foot soldiers, usually from a single manor, who assembled for military service.

secular clergy: In the Middle Ages, priests who ran local parishes, their bishops, and other standard churchmen who ministered to the public.

serf: An agricultural worker tied to a lord's land and bound to serve him for life.

steward (or **seneschal**): The general supervisor of a lord's estate and/or household.

summons: A call to military service issued by a lord to his vassals.

troubadour: A minstrel, musician, or singer who composed and/or performed songs in public and private settings.

vassal (or **retainer**): In the feudal system, a follower to whom a king or other high-ranking lord granted the use of revenue-producing land (a fief or fee) in return for fealty (loyalty) and military service.

For More Information

Books

Timothy Levi Biel, *The Age of Feudalism.* San Diego, CA: Lucent, 1994. A broad and easy-to-read overview of the political and social aspects of medieval times, including lords, serfs, vassals, manors, and knights.

Will Fowler, *Ancient Weapons: The Story of Weaponry and Warfare Through the Ages.* New York: Lorenz, 1999. Written for young people, this is a fascinating journey through the history of warfare, with hundreds of excellent color drawings and diagrams.

Joseph Gies and Frances Gies, *Life in a Medieval City.* New York: Harper & Row, 1981. An enlightening study of the people and institutions of Europe's towns and cities during the Middle Ages.

Christopher Gravett, *Knight.* New York: Knopf, 1993. Explains what medieval knights wore, their weapons, training, and battle tactics.

Barbara A. Hanawalt, *The Middle Ages: An Illustrated History.* New York: Oxford University Press, 1998. A well-organized, well-written, and nicely illustrated overview of the main historical events of the Middle Ages.

Joann Jovinelly and Jason Netelkos, *The Crafts and Culture of the Vikings.* New York: Rosen, 2002. Tells about the many colorful and often peculiar aspects of everyday life in a culture that produced some of medieval Europe's greatest warriors.

Andrew Langley, *Da Vinci & His Times.* New York: DK, 2006. An informative, very colorfully illustrated volume covering the life and accomplishments of one of the greatest geniuses who ever lived.

Web Sites

Medieval Life & the Hundred Years War (www.hyw.com/books/history/1_Help_C.htm). Two noted military historians present a huge collection of fascinating information about various aspects of medieval warfare in a format very accessible to students and general readers alike.

The Medieval Manor (http://mars.wnec.edu/~grempel/courses/wc1/lectures/22manor.html). A college professor explains in a straightforward, easy-to-understand manner how a medieval manor worked, including peasants and serfs, farming, the social classes, and life on a manor.

Medieval Monks, History for Kids (www.historyforkids.org/learn/mediev al/people/monks.htm). A useful over- view of religious people in the Mid- dle Ages, with several links to related topics.

Medieval Women, McMaster University (www.mw.mcmaster.ca/home.html). An excellent site that uses pictures, graph- ics, music, text, and more to present an entertaining overview of what life was like for women in the Middle Ages.

Index

Picture Credits

Cover: The Art Archive/British Library

Biblioteca Estense, Modena, Italy/Giraudon/ The Bridgeman Art Library, 71

Bibliotheque de L'Arsenal, Paris/Giraudon/ The Bridgeman Art Library, 63

Bibliotheque Historique de la Ville de Paris, Paris/Archives Charmet/ The Bridgeman Art Library, 70, 74, 79

Bibliotheque Mazarine, Paris/The Bridgeman Art Library, 84

Bibliotheque Municipale, Castres, France/ Giraudon/The Bridgeman Art Library, 78, 87

Bibliotheque Municipale, Rouen, France/ Giraudon/The Bridgeman Art Library, 88

Bibliotheque Nationale, Paris/Archives Charmet/The Bridgeman Art Library, 11

Bibliotheque Nationale, Paris/The Bridgeman Art Library, 62

Courtesy of the Trustees of the Sir John Soane's Museum, London/The Bridgeman Art Library, 51

Galleria dell' Accademia, Florence, Italy/ The Bridgeman Art Library, 46, 49

Galleria Sabauda, Turin, Italy/Alinari/The Bridgeman Art Library, 89

Huntington Library and Art Gallery, San Marino, CA/The Bridgeman Art Library, 53

John Bethell/The Bridgeman Art Library, 21

Maison Jeanne d'Arc, Orleans, France/The Bridgeman Art Library, 57

Musee Conde, Chantilly, France/Giraudon/ The Bridgeman Art Library, 12, 64

Museo Correr, Venice, Italy/The Bridgeman Art Library, 75, 76

Museo Lazaro Galdiano, Madrid/The Bridgeman Art Library, 47

National Gallery, London/The Bridgeman Art Library, 41, 90

Private Collection/The Bridgeman Art Library, 61

Private Collection, Archive Charmet/The Bridgeman Art Library, 59

Private Collection, © Bonhams, London/ The Bridgeman Art Library, 54

Private Collection, The Stapleton Collection/ The Bridgeman Art Library, 38

Steve Zmina, 26

The Art Archive, 15, 22

The Art Archive/Biblioteca Nazionale/ Mariciana Venice/Dagli Orti, 18, 29, 33, 37

The Art Archive/Bodleian Library, Oxford, England, 20

The Art Archive/Musee du Louvre, Paris/ Dagli Orti, 31

The Art Archive/Real Biblioteca do lo Escorial/Dagli Orti, 39

The Art Archive/The British Library, 30

The British Library/The Bridgeman Art Library, 9, 16, 17, 24, 34, 44, 58, 65, 66, 83, 85

Topkapi Palace Museum, Istanbul, Turkey/ The Bridgeman Art Library, 82

Vatican Museums and Galleries, Vatican City, Italy/The Bridgeman Art Library, 52

About the Author

Historian Don Nardo has published many volumes for young readers about ancient and medieval civilizations, including *The Roman Empire*, *A Travel Guide to Ancient Alexandria*, *The Etruscans*, *Empires of Mesopotamia*, *The Byzantine Empire*, *Life on a Medieval Pilgrimage*, and *Weapons and Warfare of the Middle Ages*. He lives in Massachusetts with his wife, Christine.